THE
EVERYTHING
PREGNANCY
ORGANIZER
2ND EDITION

THE

EVERYTHING®

PREGNANCY ORGANIZER

2ND EDITION

Monthly calendars, charts,
checklists, and schedules

Paula Ford-Martin

Adams Media
Avon, Massachusetts

Publishing Director: Gary M. Krebs
Associate Managing Editor: Laura M. Daly
Associate Copy Chief: Brett Palana-Shanahan
Acquisitions Editor: Kate Burgo
Development Editor: Rachel Engelson
Associate Production Editor: Casey Ebert

Director of Manufacturing: Susan Beale
Associate Director of Production: Michelle Roy Kelly
Cover Design: Paul Beatrice, Erick DaCosta, Matt LeBlanc
Layout and Graphics: Brewster Brownville, Colleen Cunningham, Jennifer Oliveira

Published by Adams Media, an F+W Publications Company
57 Littlefield Street
Avon, MA 02322
www.adamsmedia.com

ISBN 10: 1-59337-639-1
ISBN 13: 978-1-59337-639-0

Printed in China.

J I H G F E D C B A

This publication is designed to provide accurate and authoritative information with regard to the subject matter covered. It is sold with the understanding that the publisher is not engaged in rendering legal, accounting, or other professional advice. If legal advice or other expert assistance is required, the services of a competent professional person should be sought.
—From a *Declaration of Principles* jointly adopted by a Committee of the American Bar Association and a Committee of Publishers and Associations

Many of the designations used by manufacturers and sellers to distinguish their product are claimed as trademarks. Where those designations appear in this book and Adams Media was aware of a trademark claim, the designations have been printed with initial capital letters.

This book is available at quantity discounts for bulk purchases.
For information, please call 1–800–872–5627.

Interior illustrations by Michelle Dorenkamp

Contents

Introduction / ix

Part 1: Getting Ready / 1
Choosing a Healthcare Provider 2
Referrals... 5
Healthcare Provider Interior Sheet 8
Early Pregnancy Nutrition 13
Common Tests.. 14
Personal Medical History Worksheet 16
Family Medical History Worksheet..................... 21

Months One Through Nine
Part 2: Month One / 23
Month One Checklist 24
Your Baby This Month.................................. 24
Your Body's Changes 25
On Your Mind 28
At the Doctor's or Midwife's Office..................... 28
Prenatal Visit Notes 29
When to Contact Your Doctor or Midwife 31
Checking the Budget 32
Milestones 33
Journal 34

Part 3: Month Two / 39
Month Two Checklist 40
Your Baby This Month.................................. 40
Your Body's Changes 41
On Your Mind 41
At the Doctor's or Midwife's Office..................... 42
Prenatal Visit Notes 43
Dressing for Two 44
Modifying Your Living Space 46
Car Safety.. 48
Milestones 51
Journal 52

Part 4: Month Three / 57
Month Three Checklist 58
Your Baby This Month. 58
Your Body's Changes 58
On Your Mind 60
At the Doctor's or Midwife's Office. 61
Prenatal Visit Notes 62
Milestones 63
Journal 64

Part 5: Month Four / 69
Month Four Checklist 70
Your Baby This Month. 70
Your Body's Changes 70
Food Log 72
On Your Mind 73
At the Doctor's or Midwife's Office. 73
Prenatal Visit Notes 74
Movement!. 75
Exercise 76
Exercise Class Information 77
Spreading the Word. 79
People to Tell Early 80
Working Through Pregnancy. 82
Career Future Sheet. 84
Career Goals 86
Maternity Leave. 87
Benefits Paperwork Checklist 91
Maternity Leave Planner 92
Milestones 93
Journal 94

Part 6: Month Five / 99
Month Five Checklist 100
Your Baby This Month. 100
Your Body's Changes 100
On Your Mind 104
At the Doctor's or Midwife's Office. 105
Prenatal Visit Notes 106
Childbirth Classes 107

Childbirth Class Follow-Up Sheet. 112
Touring the Hospital/Birthing Center .114
Milestones 115
Journal 116

Part 7: Month Six / 121
Month Six Checklist 122
Your Baby This Month. 122
Your Body's Changes 122
On Your Mind 124
Prenatal Visit Notes 125
At the Doctor's or Midwife's Office. 126
Birth Plan Checklist 126
Thinking of Names. 130
Baby Names—Boys 131
Baby Names—Girls 132
Milestones 133
Journal 134

Part 8: Month Seven / 139
Month Seven Checklist 140
Your Baby This Month. 140
Your Body's Changes 140
On Your Mind 143
At the Doctor's or Midwife's Office. 143
Prenatal Visit Notes 144
Choosing a Pediatrician 145
Arranging Child Care 146
Milestones 149
Journal 150

Part 9: Month Eight / 155
Month Eight Checklist 156
Your Baby This Month. 156
Your Body's Changes 157
On Your Mind 158
At the Doctor's or Midwife's Office. 158
Prenatal Visit Notes 159
Nesting. 160
The Diaper Debate 160
Cloth Diaper Service Research 162

Postpartum Planning. 163
Milestones 167
Journal 168

Part 10: Month Nine / 173
Month Nine Checklist. 174
Your Baby This Month. 174
Your Body's Changes 174
On Your Mind 176
At the Doctor's or Midwife's Office. 176
Prenatal Visit Notes 177
Gearing Up for the Big Event 178
Packing Your Bag. 179
Outfitting Your Baby 182
Items for Leaving the House 183
Alerting Family and Friends 184
Birth Announcement Contact Sheet 185
Labor Time Checklist for Your Partner. 188
Baby Gifts 189
Labor and Delivery 192
Milestones 193
Journal 194

The Postpartum Period
Part 11: Bringing Baby Home / 199
Your Body Postpartum. 200
Recovering after Caesarean 201
Your Baby's Body 202
Breast or Bottle?. 204
Postpartum Depression 208
Thyroid Problems 209
Don't Forget to Have Fun 210
Postpartum Doctor's Visit 211
Journal 212

Appendix A: Frequently Asked Questions / 217
Appendix B: Important Contact Information / 231

Ten Month Calendar
Appendix C: Ten Month Calendar / 247
Appendix D: Estimated Due Date Table / 289

Introduction

You just found out you're pregnant. Perhaps you've been trying for just a few months, or maybe for a few years. There's also a good chance this baby has taken you by surprise; about half of all pregnancies among American women are unintended. Planned or unplanned, pregnancy stirs up a wide spectrum of emotions. You may be on cloud nine and picking out nursery patterns, or you may be in a state of shock and wondering how you're going to handle it all.

Relax. You're normal! Everyone reacts to the joys and jeopardies of pregnancy differently. Preparing yourself for the road ahead is the best way to overcome your fears and get a realistic picture of what pregnancy, and motherhood, is made of. So ask questions, read up, take classes, and talk to friends and family members who have been there. There's no such thing as too much information when it comes to your (and your baby's) health.

This organizer is designed to be a companion on your journey toward motherhood that will help you keep track of all of the information you are acquiring and allow you to breathe easy knowing that you've got it all under control.

The Everything® Pregnancy Organizer is broken down into sections by month. Each month features a checklist of tasks to take on that month, a description of how your baby is developing, an explanation of how your body is changing, a discussion of what might be on your mind, and hints on what to expect at your doctor's or midwife's visit. Each monthly section features a place to record milestones for the month and includes space for you to record your thoughts and feelings as you look ahead toward the rest of your pregnancy and your rapidly approaching life as a mom. By arming yourself with information, staying organized, and recording the multitude of feelings you will experience as you journey through your pregnancy, you will be able to fully enjoy the emotional and physical changes that make up the experience of becoming a mother.

Congratulations, and best wishes for a happy, healthy pregnancy!

Part 1

Getting Ready

After you've confirmed the good news that you're pregnant, you can begin to prepare for your pregnancy and beyond. You'll need to research healthcare provider options (from traditional to alternative practitioners), choose a healthcare provider, and begin taking prenatal vitamins to provide your baby with a healthy start.

Choosing a Healthcare Provider

Even if you have a picture-perfect pregnancy, you will be seeing a lot of your healthcare provider over the next nine months. The American College of Obstetricians and Gynecologists (ACOG) recommends that women see their providers:

- Every four weeks through the first twenty-eight weeks of pregnancy (about seven months)
- Once every two to three weeks between twenty-nine and thirty-six weeks
- Every week after thirty-six weeks

If you have any conditions that put you in a high-risk category, such as diabetes or a history of preterm labor, your provider may want to see you more frequently to monitor your progress.

Who should guide you on this odyssey? If you currently see a gynecologist or family practice doctor who also has an obstetric practice, he or she may be a good choice. If you don't have that choice, or would like to explore your options, consider the following health care professionals.

- **Ob-gyn:** An obstetrician and gynecologist is a medical doctor (M.D.) who has received specialized training in women's health and reproductive medicine.
- **Perinatologist:** If you have a chronic health condition, you may see a perinatologist—an ob-gyn who specializes in overseeing high-risk pregnancies.
- **Midwife:** There are certified nurse-midwives licensed to practice in all fifty states. They provide patient-focused care throughout pregnancy, labor, and delivery.
- **Nurse practitioner:** A nurse practitioner (N.P.) is a registered nurse (R.N.) with advanced medical education and training (at minimum, a master's degree).
- **Combined practice:** Some obstetric practices blend midwives, N.P.s, and M.D.s, with the choice (or sometimes the requirement) of seeing one or more throughout your pregnancy.

A doula is a pregnancy and birth support person, who cannot replace any of the above professionals, but who can provide emotional assistance to both the mom-to-be and her family. Doulas can assist you at any point in pregnancy, from preconception to postpartum. Because doulas tend to work with a variety of physicians and midwives in many different settings, they may also be helpful in providing information on places and providers as you plan your birth experience.

Whether it's your first or your fifth, this pregnancy is a one-time-only performance. You deserve the best support in seeing it through. Talk to the experts and get referrals. Ask for referrals from the following.

- Friends
- Family members
- State or county medical board
- Patient services department of nearby hospitals and/or birthing centers
- Labor and delivery programs of nearby hospitals and/or birthing centers
- Medical centers
- The American College of Obstetricians and Gynecologists (*www.acog.org*)
- The American College of Nurse-Midwives (*www.midwife.org*)

Be aware that not everyone looks for the same thing in a health-care provider; what another woman loves, you may cringe at.

On the following worksheets, record information about referrals that you gleaned from your contacts and/or local medical facilities and organizations.

Referrals

Healthcare professional's name
....

Position
....

Telephone number
....

Address
....

Referred by
....

Covered by your health insurance?
....

Healthcare professional's name
....

Position
....

Telephone number
....

Address
....

Referred by
....

Covered by your health insurance?
....

Healthcare professional's name
....

Position
....

Telephone number
....

Address
....

Referred by
....

Covered by your health insurance?
....

Healthcare professional's name

Position

Telephone number

Address

Referred by

Covered by your health insurance?

Healthcare professional's name

Position

Telephone number

Address

Referred by

Covered by your health insurance?

Healthcare professional's name

Position

Telephone number

Address

Referred by

Covered by your health insurance?

Referrals

Healthcare professional's name
....

Position
....

Telephone number
....

Address
....

Referred by
....

Covered by your health insurance?
....

Healthcare professional's name
....

Position
....

Telephone number
....

Address
....

Referred by
....

Covered by your health insurance?
....

Healthcare professional's name
....

Position
....

Telephone number
....

Address
....

Referred by
....

Covered by your health insurance?
....

Healthcare Provider Interview Sheet

Once you've collected names and numbers and narrowed down your list of potential providers, talk with your partner about your biggest questions, concerns, and expectations. Then compile a list of interview questions. You could photocopy the interview question sheet below and record answers for each healthcare professional you are considering as your pregnancy guide.

What are the costs and payment options? If your health plan doesn't provide full coverage, find out how much the remaining fees will run and if installment plans are available.

....

....

....

....

....

....

....

....

....

....

....

....

....

Who will deliver my baby? Will the doctor or midwife you select deliver your child, or will it be another provider in the practice, depending on when the baby arrives? If your provider works alone, find out who covers patients during vacations and emergencies.

....

....

....

....

....

....

....

Who will I see during office visits? Group practices typically share delivery responsibilities, so you may want to ask about rotating your prenatal appointments among all the providers in the group so you'll see a familiar face in the delivery room when the big day arrives.

....

....

....

....

....

....

....

Healthcare Provider Interview Sheet

What is your philosophy on routine IVs, episiotomies, labor induction, pain relief, and other interventions in the birth process? If you have certain expectations regarding medical interventions during labor and delivery, you should lay them out now.

....

....

....

....

....

....

What hospital or birthing center will I go to? Find out where the provider has hospital privileges and ask for more information on that facility's programs and policies. Ask if a neonatal unit is available if problems arise after the baby's birth. Many hospitals offer tours of their labor and delivery rooms for expectant parents.

....

....

....

....

....

....

....

What is your policy on birth plans? Will the provider work with you to create and, more important, follow a birth plan? Will the plan be signed and become part of your permanent chart in case he or she is off-duty during the birth? (For more on birth plans, see Part 7.)

....

....

....

....

....

....

How are phone calls handled if I have a health concern or question? Most obstetric practices have some sort of triage (or prioritizing) system in place for patient phone calls. Find out how quickly calls are returned and if your provider will be available to speak to if necessary. And since babies don't keep bankers' hours, find out what system they have in place for handling night and weekend patient calls.

....

....

....

....

....

....

Healthcare Provider Interview Sheet

Additional questions to ask potential providers:

....

....

....

....

....

....

....

....

....

....

....

....

....

....

....

Some providers have the staff to answer these sorts of inquiries over the phone, whereas for others you might need to schedule a face-to-face appointment with the doctor or midwife you are considering.

Early Pregnancy Nutrition

In pregnancy, a woman requires an extra 300 calories above her normal daily intake to meet the needs of her growing baby. The quality of those calories is particularly important; your developing child requires an extra boost of a variety of vitamins and minerals.

Recommended Daily Intake of Nutrients in Pregnancy (for women aged 19–50)

Calcium . . . . 1000 mg

Copper. . . . . 1000 mcg

Folate . . . . 600 mcg

Iodine . . . . 220 mcg

Iron . . . . 27 mg

Magnesium . . . . 350–360 mg

Niacin. . . . . 18 mg

Protein . . . . 50 g

Riboflavin . . . . 1.4 mg

Selenium . . . . 60 mcg

Thiamin. . . . . 1.4 mg

Vitamin A . . . . 770 mcg

Vitamin B6 . . . . 1.9 mg

Vitamin B12 . . . . 2.6 mcg

Vitamin C . . . . 85 mg

Vitamin E . . . . 15 mg

Vitamin K . . . . 90 mcg

Zinc. . . . . 11 mg

Source: Food and Nutrition Board, Institute of Medicine, National Academy of Sciences; *Dietary Reference Intake Tables*.

If you feel overwhelmed by the thought of logging every item that passes your lips, don't worry. Take your prenatal supplement as prescribed by your doctor or midwife to bank those vitamins and minerals, then follow the United States Department of Agriculture (USDA) food guide pyramid serving suggestions as a minimum guide for a balanced, healthy diet.

Common Tests

Over the course of your pregnancy, you'll be visiting your health-care provider quite a bit. Your provider will administer a number of tests to make sure that you and your baby remain healthy throughout your pregnancy, and that neither you nor your baby are at risk for complications.

Following are the most common tests you will undergo and what they test for.

Urine culture
Tests for presence of ketones and levels of protein, bacteria, and glucose

Rh factor *(Rh positive or negative)*
If you are Rh negative, you are at risk for Rh incompatibility with the blood type of your baby

Hemoglobin/hematocrit
Tests for anemia

Glucose challenge test *(GDM)*
Tests for gestational diabetes mellitus

Oral glucose tolerance test *(GTT)*
Provides definitive diagnosis of GDM

Hepatitis B
Tests for the presence of Hepatitis B in the blood

Pap smear
Detects cervical cancer, precancerous cells, vaginal infections, or inflammation of the cervix

Chorionic villus sampling *(CVS)*
Tests for Down syndrome and more than 200 other disorders

Alpha-fetoprotein (*AFP*) blood tests *(or variations called the triple or quad AFP screens)*
Screens for chromosomal irregularities like trisomy 18 and Down syndrome, and for neural tube defects

Cystic fibrosis screening
Screens to see if you are a carrier

Amniocentesis
Diagnoses chromosomal abnormalities, genetic disorders, and birth defects

Ultrasounds
May be used to diagnose placental abnormalities, an ectopic pregnancy, or certain birth defects

Personal Medical History Worksheet

Fill out your personal medical history here so you can easily answer the questions your doctor asks you at your first visit.

Chronic illnesses:

....

....

....

....

Current medications:

....

....

....

....

Current vitamins, dietary supplements, and herbal supplements:

....

....

....

....

....

Fill out your personal medical history here so you can easily answer the questions your doctor asks you at your first visit.

Allergies to medications:

....

....

....

Past surgeries:

....

....

....

Tobacco use (include frequency of use):

....

Average number of alcoholic beverages consumed per week:

....

Current level of physical activity:

....

....

Fill out your personal medical history here so you can easily answer the questions your doctor asks you at your first visit.

Have you had:	Yes	No
Seizure disorder	○	○
Epilepsy	○	○
Insomnia	○	○
Frequent anxiety	○	○
Frequent depression	○	○
Recurrent headache	○	○
Asthma	○	○
Pain/pressure in chest	○	○
Chronic cough	○	○
Palpitations (heart)	○	○
Valvular, congenital, or other heart disease	○	○
High or low blood pressure	○	○
Rheumatic fever or heart murmur	○	○
Back problems	○	○
Tumor, cancer, cyst	○	○
Jaundice (liver disease)	○	○
Stomach or intestinal trouble	○	○
Mononucleosis	○	○
Gallbladder trouble or gallstones	○	○
Recurrent diarrhea	○	○
Hernia	○	○
Recent weight gain/loss	○	○
Dizziness, fainting	○	○
Weakness, paralysis	○	○
Blood clots	○	○
Thyroid disorders	○	○

Fill out your personal medical history here so you can easily answer the questions your doctor asks you at your first visit.

Have you had:	Yes	No
Urinary tract infections or kidney disease	O	O
Bowel disease	O	O
Significant hemorrhoids	O	O
Blood transfusion	O	O
Albumin-sugar in urine	O	O
Blood in urine	O	O
Diabetes	O	O
Peptic ulcer	O	O
Collagen disease	O	O
Pneumonia	O	O
Irregular periods	O	O
Severe cramps	O	O
Excessive menstrual flow	O	O

Sexually Transmitted Diseases   Treatment
(past and present, if any)

....

....

Fertility issues *(if any)*   Treatment

....

....

Fill out your personal medical history here so you can easily answer the questions your doctor asks you at your first visit.

Number of previous pregnancies: _____

In previous pregnancy, have you experienced:	Yes	No
Birth weights less than 2,500 grams	O	O
Birth weights greater than 4,000 grams	O	O
Preterm labor	O	O
Preterm rupture of membranes before onset of labor	O	O
Complications with labor or delivery	O	O
Pregnancy-induced hypertension	O	O
Preeclampsia	O	O
Eclampsia	O	O
Postpartum hemorrhage	O	O
Third-trimester bleeding	O	O
Anemia	O	O
Miscarriage	O	O
Stillbirth	O	O
Abortion	O	O
Neonatal death	O	O

Previous miscarriage or abortion   Date of miscarriage or abortion

....

....

Other complications during   Treatments
previous pregnancies

....

....

Family Medical History Worksheet

Fill out your family medical history here so you can easily answer the questions your doctor asks you at your first visit.

Medical Condition	No	Yes	Do Not Know	Relationship
Diabetes	○	○	○	_____
Hypertension	○	○	○	_____
Psychiatric disorders	○	○	○	_____
Alcoholism	○	○	○	_____
Neural tube defects	○	○	○	_____
Multiple births	○	○	○	_____
Macrosomia	○	○	○	_____
Congenital defects	○	○	○	_____
Hearing problems	○	○	○	_____
Cleft palate or lip	○	○	○	_____
Sickle cell anemia	○	○	○	_____
Hemophilia	○	○	○	_____
Down syndrome	○	○	○	_____
Cystic fibrosis	○	○	○	_____
Huntington's Chorea	○	○	○	_____
Cerebral palsy	○	○	○	_____
Muscular dystrophy	○	○	○	_____
Nerve-muscle disorder	○	○	○	_____
Thyroid disorder	○	○	○	_____
Other hormonal disorder	○	○	○	_____
Dwarfism	○	○	○	_____
Hepatitis B, C, or carrier	○	○	○	_____
Blindness, visual problems	○	○	○	_____
Hand or feet abnormalities	○	○	○	_____

Fill out your family medical history here so you can easily answer the questions your doctor asks you at your first visit.

Medical Condition	No	Yes	Do Not Know	Relationship
Autism	○	○	○	_____
Miscarriage	○	○	○	_____
Lou Gehrig's Disease	○	○	○	_____
Cancer	○	○	○	_____
Endometriosis	○	○	○	_____
Sudden infant death syndrome	○	○	○	_____

Other

•
....
....
....
....
....
....
....
....
....
....
....

Months One
Through Nine

Part 2

Month One

During the first trimester of pregnancy, which lasts approximately fourteen weeks from the first day of your last menstrual period, your body is hard at work forming one of the most intricate and complex works of nature. By the end of your first official month of pregnancy (six weeks after your last menstrual period, but four weeks since conception), your developing child will have grown an astonishing 10,000 times in size.

Month One Checklist

✓ Evaluate your doctor, midwife, or group practice and decide if it's right for you and your pregnancy.
✓ Discuss any possible on-the-job hazards with your doctor or midwife.
✓ Evaluate your diet and begin taking prenatal vitamins if recommended by your doctor or midwife.
✓ Get up to speed on your health insurance coverage for prenatal visits, delivery, and the care of your child.
✓ If you smoke or drink, quit now.
✓ Prepare a budget to save for when your baby arrives.

Your Baby This Month

Making its longest journey until the big move nine months from now, your developing baby (called a zygote, or fertilized ovum) travels from the fallopian tube and into the uterus (or womb). By day four, the zygote has formed a small solid cluster of cells known as a morula.

By day five or six, the morula grows to a blastocyst. Within days, the blastocyst nestles into the nutrient-rich lining of your uterus (the endometrium) as implantation begins. About fifteen days after conception, the blastocyst becomes an embryo. Next to the embryo floats the yolk sac, a cluster of blood vessels that provide blood for the embryo at this early stage until the placenta takes over.

As month one draws to a close, your baby's heart is beating, lung buds have appeared, and construction of the gastrointestinal system and liver are underway. The neural tube, the basis of the baby's central nervous system, has developed and the forebrain, midbrain, and hindbrain are defined. He (or she) is starting to look more like a person, too. Arm and leg buds—complete with the beginnings of both feet and hands—are visible. It's an amazing list of accomplishments considering your baby is about the size of a raisin (less than ¼ inch long).

Your Body's Changes

At this point in your pregnancy, you might not notice any significant changes in shape and size. You may feel some of the following changes, though. Note which you are experiencing so you can look back on the progress of your pregnancy and discuss any concerns you have with your healthcare provider.

___ You feel slightly bloated, and your waistband begins to feel a bit snug.

___ Your breasts are starting to increase in size.

___ The areolas around your nipples enlarge and darken.

___ Your breasts are more tender.

___ Vaginal secretions increase, similar to those you get premenstrually.

___ You may feel tired and run down. (Grab a nap during the day or make an early bedtime a priority.)

___ You may feel faint or dizzy. (Sit or lay down on your side as soon as possible. Try not to lay flat on your back as this can make the dizziness worse.)

Morning Sickness

About three quarters of pregnant women have morning sickness during their first trimesters. Called nausea and vomiting of pregnancy (NVP) by the medical profession, morning sickness is arguably the most debilitating and prevalent of pregnancy symptoms. While most women find that morning sickness subsides or stops as the first trimester ends, for some it continues into the second and even third trimester. The following treatments have been associated with some success in lessening morning sickness in clinical trials.

Eat ginger. Ginger snaps and other foods and teas that contain ginger (*Zingiber officinale*) may be helpful in settling your stomach.

Try acupressure. Sometimes used to ward off motion sickness and seasickness, acupressure wristbands called Sea-Bands place pressure on what is called the P6, or Nei-Kuan, acupressure point. Available at most drugstores, they are an inexpensive and noninvasive way to treat morning sickness.

Consider B vitamins. Vitamin B1 (otherwise known as thiamin) and vitamin B6 have reduced morning sickness symptoms in several clinical trials. It has been suggested that morning sickness is a sign of B vitamin deficiency. Talk with your doctor or midwife before taking any supplements.

Eat smaller, more frequent meals. An empty stomach produces acid that can make you feel worse. Low blood sugar causes nausea.

Choose proteins and complex carbohydrates. Protein-rich foods—such as yogurt and beans—and complex carbs—such as baked potatoes and whole grain breads—are good for the two of you and may calm your stomach.

Eat what you like. Most pregnant women have at least one food aversion. If broccoli turns your stomach, don't force it. The better foods look and taste, the more likely they are to stay down.

Drink plenty of fluids. Don't get dehydrated. If you're vomiting, you need to replace those lost fluids. Some women report better tolerance of beverages if they are taken between meals rather than with them.

Eat juicy fruits. Turned off by water and juice right now? Try fruits like watermelon and grapes instead.

Brush regularly. Keeping your mouth fresh can cut down on the excess saliva that plagues some pregnant women and contributes to nausea. Breath mints may be helpful, too.

Talk to your provider about switching prenatal vitamins. If it makes you sick just to look at your vitamin, perhaps a chewable or other formulation will help. Iron is notoriously tough on the stomach, so your provider might also recommend a supplement with a lower or extended release amount.

Morning Sickness Survival Kit

If your stomach won't behave but you have to commute to work or elsewhere, put together a morning sickness survival kit for the car. Include the following items:

___ Wet wipes	___ Gum or breath mints
___ Tissues	___ Large freezer-grade zipper
___ Small bottle of water	lock baggies
___ Travel-sized toothbrush	___ Just-in-case change of clothes
and toothpaste	___ Graham or soda crackers

On Your Mind

Pregnancy is a time of great anticipation as you head out into uncharted waters. Worries about the baby's health and the possibility of miscarriage are common fears early in pregnancy. Although it may be easier said than done, letting go of your anxieties, at least for a little while, is the best thing for you and your baby right now.

Here are some ways to deal with anxiety about miscarriage and stress about the pregnancy:

- Designate a certain area of your home, like your bedroom, a worry-free zone, and then stick to a vow to let your anxieties go when you are in that space.
- Use an aromatherapy candle you like to help you relax.
- Play soft music or nature sounds.
- Incorporate soothing scenery in the form of photographs and posters to relieve your anxiety.

At the Doctor's or Midwife's Office

Set up your first prenatal care visit as soon as you know you are pregnant. For now through the seventh month, you'll be seeing your provider on a monthly basis (unless you are considered high risk, in which case you may have more frequent appointments). If you still haven't chosen a provider, now is the time to do so.

Your First Visit
When you go to the doctor or midwife for your first checkup, you will likely experience the following:

Prenatal Visit Notes

Stats

Weight
....

Week of pregnancy
....

Fundal height
....

Blood pressure
....

Baby's heart rate
....

Tests

Test   *Result*

....

....

....

....

Additional Notes

....

....

....

....

1. Undergo a thorough physical examination.
2. Give a urine sample (the first of many).
3. Have blood drawn for routine lab work.
4. If you haven't had a Pap smear in the last three months, your provider may also take a vaginal swab of cells scraped from your cervix for this purpose.
5. Have your pregnancy confirmed.

Be sure to record all information about the doctors or midwives that you or your partner may need in Appendix B.

Estimating Your Due Date

Most providers determine gestational age (how far along you are) from the first day of your last menstrual period (LMP). look up your due date using the table in Appendix D: Estimated Due Date Table, or if you have a regular twenty-eight-day cycle, you can figure out your own estimated due date.

1. Take the date of your last period. _____
2. Count three months back. _____
3. Add seven days. _____
4. The resulting date, _____, is your Estimated Due Date!

For example, if your last period began on September 1, you would go back through August 1 and July 1 to June 1. Then add seven days to come up with an estimated due date of June 8. An alternate method is to count 280 days (40 weeks) from the first day of your last period.

Prenatal Nutrition

For some nutritional insurance, your doctor or midwife is likely to prescribe a prenatal vitamin containing most, if not all, of these nutrients.

___ Calcium   ___ Riboflavin   ___ Vitamin C

___ Copper   ___ Thiamin   ___ Vitamin D

___ Folic acid   ___ Vitamin A   ___ Vitamin E

___ Iron   ___ Vitamin B6   ___ Zinc

___ Magnesium   ___ Vitamin B12

When to Contact Your Doctor or Midwife

If you experience any of the following symptoms, call your doctor or midwife immediately:

- Abdominal pain and/or cramping
- Fluid or blood leaking from the vagina
- Abnormal vaginal discharge (foul-smelling, green, or yellow)
- Painful urination
- Severe headache
- Impaired vision (spots or blurring)
- Fever over 101°F
- Chills
- Excessive swelling of face and/or body
- Severe and unrelenting vomiting and/or diarrhea
- Fainting or dizziness, especially if they are accompanied by abdominal pain or bleeding (They could be symptoms of ectopic, or tubal, pregnancy, a potentially fatal condition where implantation occurs outside of the endometrial lining of the uterus, such as in the fallopian tubes.)

While a good dose of common sense should be used in contacting your doctor or midwife after hours, in most cases better safe than sorry applies. Trust your instincts. If something just doesn't feel right to you, make the call.

Checking the Budget

Worried about how to make ends meet as your family grows? Sit down with your significant other and work through a budget together. Chances are there's a lot of room for cutting back.

Suggested Activity to Cut Back On	Amount Saved per Month if Scaled Back
Movies	....
Concerts	....
Weekend getaways	....
Daily cup of coffee	....
Bottled water	....
Eating out	....

Additional Way of Saving	Amount Saved Per Month
....	....
....	....
....	....
....	....
....	....
....	....
....	....

Total Potential Savings per Month:

....

By cutting back on some of your usual entertainment and dining habits, you can save a significant amount of money and have a nest egg for when your baby arrives!

Milestones

Here is a place for you to record the thoughts, feelings, and physical changes you experience during your first month of pregnancy.

Time until due date: _____

Firsts:

....

....

....

Concerns:

....

....

....

Looking forward:

....

....

....

Questions for the doctor or midwife next month:

....

....

....

Journal

Date :   /   /

Journal

Date :   /   /

Journal

Date :   /   /

Journal

Date :   /   /

Journal

Date :   /   /

Part 3

Month Two

You've made it into month two, or weeks six through ten, of your pregnancy. By the end of this month, your baby will have outgrown her embryonic development and matured into a fetus. Your body is changing rapidly. You may start to feel pregnant now, if you didn't feel so before.

Month Two Checklist

✓ Start developing a maternity wardrobe.
✓ Make room for your baby.
✓ Create a baby-safe car environment.

Your Baby This Month

Your unborn child has now advanced from raisin to raspberry size—about a half inch in length. By the end of the month, she will be about an inch long. Your baby is lengthening and straightening from the curled form she held last month. The tail she was sporting disappears around week eight, and her closed eyes start to move from the sides of her head to their permanent location. The face is further defined by a nose and jaw, and the buds of twenty tiny baby teeth are present in the gums by week ten. The palate and vocal cords also form around this time. Important organ systems are nearly completed by the end of this second month. The right and left hemispheres of your baby's brain are fully formed, and brain cell mass grows rapidly. Soft bones begin to develop, and the liver starts to manufacture red blood cells until the bone marrow can take over the job in the third trimester.

Your Body's Changes

Check off which of the following symptoms you experience this month to look back on the progress of your pregnancy and talk to your doctor or midwife about any that make you especially uncomfortable:

___ Frequent urination
___ Tender, larger breasts
___ Increased vaginal discharge
___ Occasional dizziness or faintness
___ Indigestion or gas
___ Headaches
___ Nasal congestion and/or runny nose
___ Increased saliva

On Your Mind

Now that you're feeling more symptoms of pregnancy, the reality of impending parenthood may suddenly hit home. Understanding and recognizing your emotional changes can help you better control your stress levels and mood swings.

It's easy to get stressed out over what may seem like an overwhelming amount of preparation for your new family member. Your body is already working overtime on the development of your child; try to keep your commitments and activities at a reasonable level to prevent mental and physical overload.

As you rush to get everything "just so," remember that your little one is not going to care if the crib matches the dresser, but he will feel the effects of your excess tension. Take steps to decompress when you do feel the pressure building by practicing relaxation and meditation techniques (e.g., progressive muscle relaxation, yoga with your doctor's consent), adjustments to your work or social schedule, or carving out an hour of "me" time each evening to decompress.

At the Doctor's or Midwife's Office

If you had your preliminary appointment last month, your prenatal office visits will now start to slip into a routine. At the start of each appointment, expect to:

- Step on the scale
- Give a urine sample
- Have your blood pressure checked
- Be asked about any new or continuing pregnancy symptoms
- Have your provider feel the outside of your abdomen

Bring along that list of questions that have come up since your last visit. Write these down at the conclusion of each chapter when they come to you and your partner so they are easy to find and you won't have to rely on your memory at the office.

Prenatal Visit Notes

Stats

Weight
....

Week of pregnancy
....

Fundal height
....

Blood pressure
....

Baby's heart rate
....

Tests

Test   *Result*

....

....

....

....

Additional Notes

....

....

....

....

Dressing for Two

Finding maternity clothes that are fashionable, that fit, that grow comfortably with you, and that don't cost a fortune can be a challenge. Here are a few things to keep in mind while you develop your wardrobe:

Decide how much you want to spend. If you blow your whole clothing budget on a few items, you're going to be awfully limited in your wardrobe.

Consider your laundry threshold. Check the tags and make sure that the care instructions mesh with your lifestyle. Make sure you get enough maternity pieces so you aren't washing the same three outfits constantly.

Mix and match. Try to build on what you already own by adding pieces that will work well in a variety of combinations.

Keep your sense of style. Although maternity clothes are getting more fashionable in response to women's needs, there are still plenty of overalls festooned with ruffles and appliqués out there. Buy what you like!

Built to last? If you're planning on stretching the shelf life of your maternity clothes through another pregnancy, spending a little more on well-made, durable attire is more economical in the long run.

Purchase some nice loungewear or pajama sets. They'll be perfect for your take-it-easy days.

Think about the time of year when you'll be delivering. Especially if you live in a region with an inconsistent climate, consider how the weather will change during your pregnancy. To bridge the seasonal shifts, buy clothing that layers.

Borrow from your partner's closet. Oversized button-down oxfords, khakis, and even some of his cargo shorts can help you fill the gap in sizes from when you are not showing to when you require maternity clothes.

Ask for loans. Tap formerly pregnant friends and family for contributions.

Rent a wardrobe. There is a new breed of maternity clothing boutique, where for a monthly or weekly fee you can rent a selection of outfits to get you through pregnancy. If you're planning on a subsequent pregnancy, however, you won't have anything to keep and use again.

Check consignment shops. Because of their limited lifespan in most women's closets, maternity clothes make great resale shop fodder. Consignment stores that deal specifically in maternity wear are becoming more commonplace; check your local yellow pages to see if there is one near you.

Modifying Your Living Space

During the second month of pregnancy, start thinking about where your baby will be sleeping (or not sleeping) and playing so you can coordinate logistics and gear. If you're torn about giving up your study for a nursery (after all, she's small—how much space can she need?), think about the baby basics—crib, changing area, and dresser—plus all the inevitable stuff you're bound to acquire—swing, stuffed animals, bouncy chair, baby books, and bathtub—and the choice becomes clear.

Making Room

If a nursery isn't an option due to the size of your home or financial considerations, there are several ways to give your baby a place of her own by separating out a part of a room, including:

- Using a folding screen (or two)
- Hanging curtains from a ceiling track
- Building a wall for a more permanent partition

Nursery Safety

Evaluate the area for safety hazards. Make sure that you have:

___ No peeling paint
___ No dangling blind cords
___ No loose flooring
___ No two piece doorstoppers (the rubber bumpers on many models can be a choking hazard)
___ No decorative crib features that could potentially catch on clothing or entrap the baby
___ Crib slats that are a maximum of $2\frac{3}{8}$ inches apart
___ A mattress that fits snugly against the crib sides

Baby-proofing

Although your home safety efforts will undoubtedly pick up steam as your child gets mobile and starts exploring her surroundings, there are some basic things you can do now to protect her in infancy and beyond. Check off the following precautions as you complete them:

Register for recalls. Take the time to fill out those registration cards for all the baby gear you receive. If a safety recall of the product occurs, the manufacturer will be able to notify you. You can also register for e-mail alerts of new product recalls from the U.S. Consumer Product Safety Commission at *www.cpsc.gov.*

Ban cigarettes. You already know how dangerous it is to smoke during pregnancy, but did you know that secondhand smoke, particularly in a closed home environment, is harmful to your baby's health?

Get the lead out. Lead paint and lead solder, most frequently found in homes built before 1978, is a major hazard to small children. When ingested, it can cause central nervous system damage and developmental problems. Contact a lead inspector to test your home for the presence of lead and to advise you on abatement procedures.

Rearrange the furniture. Block off electrical cords and buy plastic protectors to seal up open outlets. Pad sharp table corners to protect your baby from injury.

Move dangerous items. Store medications, cleaning products, and plastic bags out of a child's reach.

Put the lid down. Make sure all members of the household leave the toilet seat (and lid) down. Small children are top-heavy. If they peer into the toilet, they can fall in but aren't strong enough to get out.

Evaluate your home from a baby's eye view. Crawl around your home. Pay special attention to anything about three feet off the floor and move anything dangerous, expensive, or breakable to higher ground.

Car Safety

Cast a critical eye toward your current vehicle to make sure it meets both the practical and safety concerns of your growing family. Check to make sure your current vehicle meets the following safety standards and allows you to take suggested precautions when baby arrives. If you have not checked off the entire list, record below what remains to be done to make your car baby-safe before your baby is born.

Sit back and be safe. The best place for any child is the back seat. If you have the choice, avoid pickup trucks or other vehicles that don't offer one.

Turn off the air bag. If your new baby must ride in the front passenger seat and there is an air bag, there absolutely must be a switch that allows you to disengage the air bag on that side. If your vehicle doesn't have a switch, obtain permission to install one from the National Highway Traffic Safety Administration (NHTSA). Check with your state's motor vehicle bureau for details.

Skip the side air bag. Side impact air bags can also pose a significant risk of head and neck injury to children. If the vehicle has an activated rear seat side air bag, check with the car manufacturer or the NHTSA to make sure it has been adequately tested for safe use with children. Otherwise, have it deactivated (for complete information on deactivating airbags, go to *www.safercar.gov/ airbags*).

Choose the right seat. Size and shape matter. Make sure your baby's car seat fits properly in the vehicle and there is adequate room if you have more than one child to secure. Remember your little one will ride in a rear-facing car seat until she weighs twenty pounds and is one year of age.

Use locking seat belts, tethers, or anchors. Most vehicles built after 2002 accommodate a LATCH system (lower anchors and tethers for children) that allows you to secure the top and side tethers on a LATCH equipped child seat to anchors built into the car interior. If your car seat or vehicle is not LATCH equipped, cars built after 1996 should have belts that work with most car seats. Always check the owner's manual of your vehicle and car seat for proper installation instructions.

Check the interior trunk release. If your car was manufactured after September 2001, it should have a release mechanism inside the trunk to prevent curious children from becoming trapped inside. Retrofitted release latches are available for cars without this feature.

Don't run hot and cold. If your car's heating and cooling system is out of commission, now is the time to get it fixed. You may not mind sweating in summer or freezing in winter, but an infant can quickly become overheated or chilled. The Centers for Disease Control and Prevention (CDC) recommends turning on the car's air conditioner in weather 75°F or warmer and firing up the heater when it dips below 50°F.

Accessorize. Car seat belts and buckles left in the sun can pose a burn hazard so consider a car seat cover or window and windshield sun screens, which are also useful in preventing your car's interior from absorbing the sun's heat.

Other features that may be helpful but aren't absolutely essential include built-in child car seats and safety door locks.

Milestones

Here is a place for you to record the thoughts, feelings, and physical changes you experience during your second month of pregnancy.

Time until due date: _____

Firsts:

....

....

....

Concerns:

....

....

....

Looking forward:

....

....

....

Questions for the doctor or midwife next month:

....

....

....

Journal

Date: /   /

Journal

Date :   /   /

Journal

Date: /   /

Journal

Date :   /   /

Journal

Date :   /   /

Part 4

Month Three

This is a landmark month as you finish up your first trimester! By the end of this month, your baby will grow to more than three inches in length and almost one ounce, about the size and heft of a roll of Life Savers. His head accounts for one-third of his total length, and his tongue, salivary glands, and taste buds have formed. You make first contact this month as you hear his heartbeat and perhaps even see him on ultrasound.

Month Three Checklist

✓ Create ways to compensate for forgetfulness.
✓ Make sleep a priority; set a new early bedtime and stick to it.

Your Baby This Month

Your baby's heart is pumping about twenty-five quarts of blood each day, and a lattice of blood vessels can be seen through his translucent skin, which is starting to develop a coat of fine downy hair called lanugo. His, or her, gender is apparent since the external sex organs have now fully differentiated, but it will take a combination of luck and technical skill for an ultrasound operator to reveal if you have a son or daughter.

Your Body's Changes

This month, you start to sport a protruding belly, which may mean sharing your news with friends, family, and coworkers if you haven't already. Your uterus is about the size of a softball and stretches to just about your pubic bone. Two to four pounds of total weight gain is about average for the first trimester; if you've been down and out with nausea and vomiting, you may be below the curve. Weight gain will pick up in the second trimester and peak in the third as your baby starts to fill out your womb.

While twenty-five to thirty-five pounds is the average suggested total weight gain for a pregnancy, your height and build will influence that number. Underweight women and women with multiple pregnancies (twins or more) will be expected to gain more; overweight women will be encouraged to gain slightly less.

If your provider hasn't mentioned a weight goal for your pregnancy, ask for your weight goal and record it here.

My Pregnancy Weight Goal _____

Focus on the quality of food you're eating and on getting some regular exercise (cleared with your provider first).

Where the Weight Goes

Baby	7.5 to 8.5 pounds
Uterus	2 to 2.5 pounds
Placenta	1.5 to 2 pounds
Amniotic fluid	2 pounds
Blood	3 to 4 pounds
Breasts	1 to 2 pounds
Maternal fat and nutrient stores	4 to 6 pounds
Retained maternal fluids	4 to 8 pounds
Total	**25 to 35 pounds**

Although nausea and vomiting may finally be waning, constipation, gas, and occasional heartburn may take over as the gastrointestinal pests of the second trimester.

Constipation can be caused by an increase in progesterone, which can act to slow down the digestive system. Later in the pregnancy, pressure on the intestines caused by your growing uterus adds to the problem. Iron supplements or prenatal vitamins with added iron can also cause constipation, so talking to your provider about the possibility of a dosage adjustment or an extended release formula may be in order. An increase in dietary fiber, plenty of water intake, and exercise as approved by your healthcare provider may also help to get things going again. Be sure to consult your doctor before taking any stool softeners or laxatives.

Other pregnancy symptoms that may continue or begin this month include the following. Check off symptoms you experience this month and talk to your doctor or midwife about any that make you especially uncomfortable:

___ Fatigue

___ Frequent urination

___ Tender breasts

___ Occasional dizziness or faintness

___ Headaches

___ Nasal congestion and/or runny nose

___ Increased saliva

___ Nausea

On Your Mind

Like any mom-to-be, you've got a lot on your mind. That alone may have you forgetting what used to be second nature and misplacing things. Pregnancy hormones, sleep deprivation, and stress have all been suggested as possible culprits.

Whatever the cause, forgetting appointments and misplacing things can leave you feeling muddled and helpless. To cope with forgetfulness, try the following.

- Writing notes
- Sticking to a routine (e.g., car keys always go into a basket by the door)
- Living by a written or electronic organizer
- Requesting a twenty-four-hour advance phone call reminder when you schedule appointments such as in-home appliance repair or a hair cut

At the Doctor's or Midwife's Office

This month, your provider may:

- Order an ultrasound to see your baby
- Start estimating the size of your baby by counting the centimeters from your pubic bone to the tip of your fundus—the top of the uterus (Some practitioners do not take the fundal height until after week twelve or even week twenty.)
- Tell you about the alpha-fetoprotein test (The AFP is typically given at sixteen to eighteen weeks, and it tests for the possibility of neural tube defects and/or chromosomal abnormalities. Since it is optional, many providers give an informational sheet to patients so they may consider whether they want to take it.)
- Check for the fetal heartbeat using a small ultrasound device called a Doppler or Doptone

Stats

Weight
....

Week of pregnancy
....

Fundal height
....

Blood pressure
....

Baby's heart rate
....

Tests

Test	*Result*
....	....
....	....
....	....
....	....

Additional Notes

....

....

....

....

Milestones

Here is a place for you to record the thoughts, feelings, and physical changes you experience during your third month of pregnancy.

Time until due date: _____

Firsts:

....

....

....

Concerns:

....

....

....

Looking forward:

....

....

....

Questions for the doctor or midwife next month:

....

....

....

Journal

Date :   /   /

Journal

Date :   /   /

Journal

Date :   /   /

Journal

Date :   /   /

Journal

Date: /   /

Part 5

Month Four

Welcome to the second trimester, or what many women consider the fun part. Your energy is up, and your meals are staying down. You and your baby are headed into a period of rapid growth now, so hang on and enjoy the ride.

Month Four Checklist

✓ Treat yourself to a special day out.
✓ Begin keeping a food log.
✓ If you don't have one, shop for a crib that meets current safety standards.
✓ Create a prenatal exercise routine.

Your Baby This Month

Snoozing, stretching, swallowing, and even thumb-sucking, your baby is busy this month as she tests out her new reflexes and abilities. She is losing her top-heavy look as her height starts to catch up to her head size. By the end of this month, she will measure about six to eight inches in length and weigh approximately six ounces.

Your Body's Changes

If you weren't showing last month, chances are you will have a definite pregnant profile by the end of this month. Your uterus is about the size of a head of cabbage, and its top lies just below your belly button.

Your appetite may start to pick up this month, especially if you've been too sick to enjoy a good meal until now. About 60 percent of your total pregnancy weight (about eleven to fifteen pounds) will be gained in this trimester.

Heartburn may start to become a persistent problem as your uterus crowds your stomach and the smooth muscles of your digestive tract remain relaxed from the hormone progesterone. Some tips for putting out the fire include:

- Avoid greasy, fatty, and spicy foods.
- Stay away from alcohol and caffeinated drinks (e.g., cola, tea, coffee); these may relax the valve between the stomach and the esophagus and exacerbate heartburn.
- Eat smaller, more frequent meals instead of three large ones.
- Drink plenty of water between meals to reduce stomach acid.
- Don't eat just before you go to bed or lay down to rest.
- Pile a few extra pillows on the bed to assist gravity in easing heartburn while you sleep.

Another option you have is to keep a food log to try to determine what your heartburn triggers are. On the following page is a food log page that you can photocopy to fill in each day.

Other symptoms of second-trimester pregnancy you may start or continue to experience this month include the following. Check off those that you are experiencing so that you may discuss relief with your doctor:

___ Hemorrhoids
___ Nausea
___ Fatigue
___ Frequent urination

Food Log

Food	Portion	Time Eaten	Activity Following Consumption
french fries	1 cup	3:15 P.M.	went for a walk

__ Tender and/or swollen breasts
__ Bleeding gums
__ Excess mucus and saliva
__ Increase in vaginal discharge
__ Mild shortness of breath
__ Lightheadedness or dizziness
__ Gas and/or constipation
__ Skin and hair changes
__ Feeling warm or easily overheated

On Your Mind

You're hitting your stride as the wooziness and uncertainties of the first three months fade away, and the discomforts of late pregnancy still lie relatively far ahead.

Feeling better and having more energy, you may be ready to conquer the world (or at least the nursery). For many women, the starter's pistol on motherhood goes off right when they feel baby's first pokes and prods. The palpable presence of your child may trigger a series of mothering emotions—protectiveness, nurturing, nesting—and complete and total impatience with anyone who poses a potential threat to the well-being of you and your child.

At the Doctor's or Midwife's Office

If you didn't get to listen to your baby's heartbeat last month, you'll likely get your chance with this visit. Women who have chosen to take an alpha-fetoprotein (AFP) test will have their blood drawn sometime between weeks sixteen and eighteen.

Prenatal Visit Notes

Stats

Weight
....

Week of pregnancy
....

Fundal height
....

Blood pressure
....

Baby's heart rate
....

Tests

Test	*Result*
....	....
....	....
....	....
....	....

Additional Notes

....

....

....

....

Movement!

If this is your second or third child, you may already recognize the familiar sensation of your baby's body flexing in your womb. For moms in their debut pregnancy with somewhat less stretchy accommodations, the first movements—known as quickening—may not be felt quite as early. By week nineteen, most women have felt that distinctive first flutter.

So what does it feel like? Record what those first baby movements felt like for you.

....

....

....

Once your baby starts moving regularly, the sensation becomes second nature. When you begin to feel your baby moving regularly, try to record how many movements you feel within a few hours to get an idea of your baby's average number of movements per hour.

Hour One _____
Hour Two _____
Hour Three _____

On average, you should feel four or more movements each hour from your passenger. Three or fewer movements or a sudden decrease in fetal activity could be a sign of fetal distress, so if you notice either, call your provider as soon as possible to follow up.

Exercise

Don't avoid the gym, pool, or other favorite fitness hangouts just because you're pregnant. Exercise will make you feel better, and it can tone muscles that will be getting a workout in labor and delivery (be sure, though, to check with your healthcare provider before beginning an exercise routine). For women in regular pregnancies (i.e., not high-risk), thirty minutes of moderate exercise daily is ideal. Consider the benefits a regular workout may provide:

- **Keep energy up.** Stretching and moving daily will boost your energy level.
- **Relax.** Exercise can help calm your mind.
- **Get postpartum weight down.** It will be easier to work off your pregnancy weight after the birth if you already have a regular routine.
- **Ease your aches and pains.** Exercise that promotes strength and flexibility can prevent or diminish lower back pain, muscle aches, and other complaints of pregnancy.
- **Foster a positive mental attitude.** Feeling fit may improve your self-image.

It's best to avoid exercises that can cause you to become overheated or that involve bouncing, jarring, sudden changes in direction, lifting, or a risk of falling. Here are some generally safe pregnancy exercise ideas:

Hiking	Stair climbing
Golf (sans cart)	Stationary biking
Yoga	Stretching exercises with a pregnancy ball
Swimming	Light weight lifting
Walking	Water aerobics

Consider asking the following questions before you sign up for an exercise class (such as yoga or prenatal exercise) at your gym:

Do the times of the class fit your schedule?

....

....

What is the missed-class policy?

....

....

....

Are postpartum women in the class as well? If so, does the class include different exercises for them?

....

....

....

What type of pregnancy training does the instructor have?

....

....

....

If you decide to sign up for an exercise class or multiple exercise classes, record information you may need later if you have to call and cancel your membership to the class, if you have questions for the instructor, or if you need to be reminded of the class schedule.

Class name: ....

Class location: ....

Gym phone number: ....

Gym hours: ....

Instructor: ....

Instructor contact information: ....

Class times: ....

Number of classes missed:* ....

Class name: ....

Class location: ....

Gym phone number: ....

Gym hours: ....

Instructor: ....

Instructor contact information: ....

Class times: ....

Number of classes missed: ....

Class name: ....

Class location: ....

Gym phone number: ....

Gym hours: ....

Instructor: ....

Instructor contact information: ....

Class times: ....

Number of classes missed: ....

Class name: ....

Class location: ....

Gym phone number: ....

Gym hours: ....

Instructor: ....

Instructor contact information: ....

Class times: ....

Number of classes missed: ....

*You should keep track of the number of classes you have missed if your gym has rules about the number of missed classes allowed before you are unenrolled.

Spreading the Word

Here are some ideas for sharing the news with family and friends:

- Give them an ultrasound picture (or a photocopy of one).
- Send out birthday invitations for the estimated due date.
- Take out a "Help Wanted: Grandparents" advertisement in their local classifieds and point them to it.
- Invite them to dinner (at home or out) and serve a frosting-inscribed "It's a Boy/Girl/Baby," "Congratulations Auntie," or "We're Pregnant" cake for dessert.
- Ask them to go shopping with you and take them to your four-month doctor's or midwife's appointment instead.
- If this isn't your first, let your kids spread the news in their own special way.
- The old standby—"Guess what?"—works well, too.

People to Tell Early

Here you can make a list of people you want to alert early on about your pregnancy. Consider family, friends, and coworkers.

Name:
....

Address:
....

Phone number:
....

E-mail address:
....

Name:
....

Address:
....

Phone number:
....

E-mail address:
....

Name:
....

Address:
....

Phone number:
....

E-mail address:
....

Name:
....

Address:
....

Phone number:
....

E-mail address:
....

Here you can make a list of people you want to alert early on about your pregnancy. Consider family, friends, and coworkers.

Name:
....

Address:
....

Phone number:
....

E-mail address:
....

Name:
....

Address:
....

Phone number:
....

E-mail address:
....

Name:
....

Address:
....

Phone number:
....

E-mail address:
....

Name:
....

Address:
....

Phone number:
....

E-mail address:
....

Working Through Pregnancy

Make sure that your employer hears about your pregnancy from you, and not around the water cooler, first. Accompany the news with your tentative schedule for maternity leave so your manager can plan accordingly.

If this is your first child, it can be hard to fully assess the new career direction you're taking. But there are probably some basic decisions you can make with a degree of certainty. For example, late shifts and double-overtime may be out of the picture for you now.

You should also ask questions to determine whether your company is even worth sticking with through your pregnancy and beyond. Comment in the spaces below to see how your company stacks up in the family-friendly category.

Flexibility: Does the company have written policies on options like flex-time, job-sharing, and telecommuting?

....

....

....

Lactation facilities: Are there appropriate, comfortable areas dedicated to breastfeeding or breast milk pumping? If not, is your employer willing to provide an appropriate, private space?

....

....

....

Paid paternity leave: Are dads given time off for a new baby with pay, or at least without prejudice? If a policy is in place, is it used successfully?

....

....

....

On-site child care or child care assistance: If your workplace doesn't have on-site or sponsored child care, does it offer enrollment in a tax-free flexible spending account that allows you to save up to $5,000 tax free to pay child care expenses?

....

....

....

Time-saving perks: These may run the gamut from on-site dry cleaning and retail services to employee concierge services that can run small errands for you.

....

....

....

Value placed on education: Corporate-sponsored scholarships for children of employees, tuition assistance, and mentorship programs with local schools are a few ways a company may express the value of education.

....

....

....

Ask yourself the following questions to assess the career direction you may want to take and decide what are feasible goals for your job future.

Do you want to move into a supervisory position at your next review? Do you see your company promoting people who work excessive overtime? If so, are you capable of committing to working extra hours after your baby is born?

....

....

....

Will you require an extremely or moderately flexible job?

....

....

....

Is your partner's job flexible enough to allow your job to be less so?

....

....

....

Do you intend to continue advancing in your current career so as to be the primary earner in your family, or will your partner take on that role?

....

....

....

Ask yourself the following questions to assess the career direction you may want to take and decide what are feasible goals for your job future.

Are you a single parent who will be relying on your own income after your baby is born?

....

....

....

....

Do you have options for affordable child care for when your baby is born? How does this affect your postpartum working schedule?

....

....

....

....

Is your job adaptable so that you can work from home? If not, would you like a job that is?

....

....

....

....

....

Career Goals

After completing the previous questionnaire, you can use your answers to create career goals based on what job characteristics you will be looking for once your child is born.

Career/Lifestyle Goal	How to Achieve My Goal
Have afternoons off	Become a part-time speech therapist instead of a full-time speech therapist.

Maternity Leave

It's a good idea to put all maternity leave plans in writing for your supervisor and appropriate managers and to make an extra copy for placement in your personnel file.

Lay the groundwork for your maternity leave so there won't be too many questions or crises in your absence. If appropriate for your position, delegate some tasks to coworkers and arrange coverage by others.

Check and double-check that all appropriate benefits paperwork has been filled out, signed off, and sent in well in advance of your planned departure. Maternity leave should be a low-stress time, not one that requires twice weekly contact with human resources to find out the status of your disability claim.

So just how much, or how little, maternity leave should you take? Certainly the benefits your company provides will play a major factor in your decision. Factors to consider include:

Flexibility: Does the company have written policies on options like flex-time, job-sharing, and telecommuting?

....

....

....

....

....

....

....

Money: How much time off can you afford if your maternity benefits are minimal or nonexistent? Don't forget to factor any money you'll be saving—such as dry cleaning bills, lunches out, and transportation expenses—into your equation.

....

....

....

....

....

....

....

....

Management: Even though you may be legally within your rights, in some organizations an extended maternity leave may be frowned upon by those above you. What might management think, and more important, what kind of priority do you place on their disapproval?

....

....

....

....

....

....

....

Morale: Are your coworkers and/or subordinates happy and motivated or disillusioned and bitter? Employees who work as a team and feel invested in their workplace are more likely to rise to the challenge in your absence.

....

....

....

....

....

....

....

Malleability: Does it have to be all or nothing? Think about offering some creative proposals for extending your leave, such as a reduced part-time schedule or telecommuting.

....

....

....

....

....

....

....

Full-Time at Home

Finally, for the woman who wants it all and wants it close to home, consider the possibility of forging your own family-friendly path. Many occupations lend themselves to home-based work, such as:

- Writing
- Income tax preparation
- Desktop publishing
- Web design
- Refinishing antiques
- Creating crafts for retail
- Sewing
- Painting

Additional ideas for a home-based business:

....

....

....

....

....

....

....

....

....

....

Benefits Paperwork Checklist

Necessary Form	Deadline for Submission	Date Turned In
....	....	....
....	....	....
....	....	....
....	....	....
....	....	....
....	....	....
....	....	....
....	....	....
....	....	....
....	....	....
....	....	....
....	....	....
....	....	....
....	....	....
....	....	....
....	....	....

Maternity Leave Planner

Estimated due date:
....

Employer insurance benefits offered:
....

....

....

Total leave requested:
....

Amount of paid time off:
....

Amount of unpaid time off:
....

Estimated cost of unpaid time off:
....

Replacement arrangement (temporary help, coworker replacement, etc.):

....

....

....

....

....

....

Responsibilities to take care of before leave:

....

....

....

....

Milestones

Here is a place for you to record the thoughts, feelings, and physical changes you experience during your fourth month of pregnancy.

Time until due date: _____

Firsts:

....

....

....

Concerns:

....

....

....

Looking forward:

....

....

....

Questions for the doctor or midwife next month:

....

....

....

Journal

Date :   /   /

Journal

Date :   /   /

Journal

Date :   /   /

Journal

Date : / /

Journal

Date :   /   /

Part 6

Month Five

This month, you're still enjoying the relative comfort level of the second trimester, but your energy and initiative may be slightly dampened by the dwindling quality of your sleep. Sleep deprivation can also contribute to mental fuzziness and emotional edginess. Now's the time to value and prioritize time spent sleeping.

Month Five Checklist

✓ Plan a special night out with your partner.
✓ Choose a method of childbirth instruction.
✓ Tour childbirth centers.

Your Baby This Month

At ten to twelve inches long and around a pound in weight, your baby is about the size of a football. He is starting to bulk up a bit as he accumulates deposits of brown fat under his skin. This insulation will help regulate his body temperature in the outside world. He's using his bulk to make his presence known; if you weren't feeling him last month you likely are now.

Your baby is now covered in a white oily substance known as vernix caseosa, a sort of full-body fetal ChapStick that keeps his fluid-soaked skin from peeling and protects against infection.

Your Body's Changes

As your baby grows, your muscles and ligaments stretch to support this new weight. The result may be a new set of aches and pains as your body adjusts to the load.

The skin of your belly is stretching, tightening, and itching like crazy. A good moisturizing cream can relieve the itching and keep your skin hydrated, although it won't prevent or eliminate striae gravidarum, or stretch marks.

The band of ligaments supporting your uterus is carrying an increasingly heavy load. You may start to feel occasional discomfort in your lower abdomen, inner thighs, and hips called round ligament pain. Pelvic tilt exercises are useful for keeping pelvic muscles toned and relieving pain. To perform the pelvic tilt:

1. Kneel on all fours on the floor.
2. Keeping your head aligned with your spine, pull in your abdomen, tighten your buttocks, and tilt your pelvis forward. Your back will naturally arch up.
3. Hold the position for three seconds, then relax. (Remember to keep your back straight in this neutral position.)
4. Repeat the tilt three to five times, eventually working up to ten repetitions.

The root of all things uncomfortable—pregnancy hormones—are also contributing to lower back pain you may be experiencing. Progesterone and relaxin—the hormone responsible for softening your pelvic ligaments for delivery—are also loosening up your lower back ligaments and disks, and combined with the weight of your growing belly your back is feeling the strain.

If your abdominal and/or back pains are severe or accompanied by any of the following, call your healthcare provider immediately:

• Fever
• Vomiting
• Vaginal bleeding
• Leg numbness

Most minor back pain of pregnancy is completely normal, but in severe cases it can be a sign of preterm labor, kidney infection, or other medical problems.

To help you ease your aches and pains:

Stand tall. Try to keep your center of gravity in your spine and pelvis rather than out in your belly, which can give you a swayback.

Sit up straight. Use good posture when you're sitting as well and choose a chair with good lower back support. You can purchase a special ergonomic support pad for your chair back, but a small pillow may do the trick just as easily.

Avoid twists and turns. With everything so loose, a sudden move as simple as quickly turning at the waist to get out of bed may strain your back. Use your arms as support for a slow takeoff when rising from a chair.

Practice your pickups. If you have small children who still need to be lifted occasionally, it's essential to use good form. To avoid injury, bend and use your leg muscles to lift things rather than bending from the waist and lifting with your back.

Warm up. A warm pad on your back, hips, or other sore spots may help relieve pain.

Wear sensible shoes. Avoid high heels! They will place further stress on your spine.

Rest your feet. Use a low stool or step to rest your feet when sitting. If you must stand for long periods, alternate resting each foot on a step.

Massage. You now have a medical excuse to indulge in a regular back rub from your significant other. A licensed massage therapist who is experienced in prenatal massage may also be helpful.

Fluff and stuff. Sleep on your side with a pillow placed between your legs. This will align your spine and improve your sleeping posture. A full-sized body pillow or beanbag may help support your back and belly as well.

Exercise. Stretching and flexibility exercises may help.

Symptoms you may start or continue to experience this month include the following. Check off any that you are experiencing so that you may ask your doctor about relief and to track the progress of your pregnancy.

__ Hot flashes

__ Nausea

__ Fatigue

__ Frequent urination

__ Tender and/or swollen breasts

__ Bleeding gums

__ Excess mucus and saliva

__ Increase in vaginal discharge

__ Mild shortness of breath

__ Lightheadedness or dizziness

__ Headaches

__ Gas

__ Heartburn

__ Constipation

__ Skin and hair changes

On Your Mind

If family and friends are getting your ire up, it may be a sign that you are feeling overwhelmed and undersupported. Take a look at what's really getting to you. Sit down and tell your partner what you're feeling and work out some strategies for easing the burden together. It may help to write down what you are having difficulty dealing with, then work with your partner to create a solution.

Challenge   Solution

....

....

....

....

....

....

....

....

....

....

....

Step back and take stock. Are you making work, and stress, for yourself through self-imposed deadlines? Look at your to-do list in terms of small tasks rather than an all-or-nothing prospect. Prioritize what's there and dare to cross off a few things that just aren't that important right now.

Old To-Do List	Newly Prioritized and Shortened To-Do List
....	....
....	....
....	....
....	....
....	....
....	....
....	....
....	....
....	....

At the Doctor's or Midwife's Office

Beyond the usual weigh and measure routine, your doctor or midwife may administer an oral glucose tolerance test (OGTT) at the end of the month (between weeks twenty-four and twenty-eight). If your doctor or midwife hasn't discussed counting fetal movements before, he or she may mention it now.

Stats

Weight
....

Week of pregnancy
....

Fundal height
....

Blood pressure
....

Baby's heart rate
....

Tests

Test	*Result*
....	....
....	....
....	....
....	....

Additional Notes

....

....

....

....

Childbirth Classes

Now's a good time to start gathering information on childbirth classes from your local hospital or birthing center. There are several different methods of childbirth education, such as Lamaze, the Bradley Method, Leboyer, and HypnoBirthing; researching them now will give you and your partner time to learn more about which one is right for you. Pick a class date that falls in your third trimester so the information will still be fresh in your mind once the big day arrives. While hospital policy will dictate a lot of what's covered in prepared childbirth classes, here's a general idea of what you will experience:

- **Commiseration:** You'll interact with other pregnant couples and demonstrate that misery (and joy) truly does love company.
- **Reality:** Through lecture and (in many cases) actual video footage, you'll get the full scoop on what really goes on in labor and delivery.
- **Guided tour:** If your class is at the birthing center or hospital, you will probably get a tour of the facilities and some basic instructions on when and where to show up when labor hits.
- **Teamwork:** Your husband, partner, or labor coach will learn more about his or her role in this process, and you may even be given homework to try out techniques at home.
- **After-birth instruction:** Many classes offer valuable information on breastfeeding basics and baby care. Don't be surprised if the instructor brings in a bag full of baby dolls for practice.
- **Seasoned support:** Most prepared childbirth classes will be conducted by a trained childbirth educator.
- **Paperwork:** A lot of literature, brochures, pamphlets, handouts, forms, photocopies, and leaflets will come your way. Bring a bag.

To find out which method is right for you, explore the details of each in the following sections.

Lamaze

While rhythmic breathing exercises are stressed for each stage of labor in Lamaze, helpful laboring and birth positions, relaxation techniques, and pain management are also covered. In addition to massage, water therapy, and hot and cold compresses, you're taught how to focus on a picture or object to diminish your discomfort.

Lamaze also stresses the empowerment of the mother-to-be and her right to the birth experience and environment she wants.

Pros   Cons

....

....

....

....

....

....

....

Additional Thoughts

....

....

....

....

Bradley Method

Denver obstetrician Robert Bradley, M.D., was a big advocate of fathers helping their partners through the birth process. Bradley Method classes teach couples how to relax and breathe deeply, but the emphasis is on doing what comes naturally—such as father as coach, proper nutrition during pregnancy, and knowing all the options beforehand. They also emphasize the *natural* in natural childbirth, suggesting that pain medication be used as a last resort rather than a front-line tool.

Pros

Cons

....

....

....

....

....

....

....

Additional Thoughts

....

....

....

....

Leboyer

Frederick Leboyer, M.D., author of *Birth without Violence*, developed this method of childbirth that attempts to soften the trauma of the transition from the warm, dark womb to the cold, bright world. It advocates dim lights in the delivery room, a warm bath for the new baby, calm voices, and soothing room temperatures.

Pros   **Cons**

....

....

....

....

....

....

....

....

Additional Thoughts

....

....

....

....

HypnoBirthing

British doctor and natural childbirth pioneer Grantly Dick-Read, who authored the classic *Childbirth without Fear*, is the inspiration behind HypnoBirthing education. Dr. Dick-Read believed that a woman's labor pains were magnified by her fear and anxieties. HypnoBirthing emphasizes slow abdominal breathing and other relaxation techniques that teach you how to focus on the feelings and signals your body sends during labor.

Pros   Cons

....

....

....

....

....

....

....

Additional Thoughts

....

....

....

....

Childbirth Class Follow-Up Sheet

If you are still confused about different types of childbirth classes, call your hospital or birthing center and ask for printed schedules and descriptions of upcoming classes. Once you get a basic feel for what is offered, you can call with follow-up questions. Use the template below to gain as much information as you can.

What are the instructor's credentials and training?

....

What methods are taught in the class?

....

What is the typical class size?

....

What does the curriculum consist of?

....

How much does enrollment cost?

....

Are there additional costs beyond the enrollment fee, such as for study materials or learning aids?

....

Are there couples that can be contacted as references?

....

....

....

Once you have chosen which class best suits your needs and those of your partner, record any information about the class here.

Class starting date:
....

Class meeting times:
....

Class instructor:
....

Address of class:
....

Phone number of facility:
....

Additional notes:
....

....

....

When you begin taking labor classes later in your pregnancy, use this space to record notes from class. As you approach the time of labor, you can check back and review the helpful tips and techniques that you learned in childbirth class.

....

....

....

....

....

....

....

....

....

Touring the Hospital/Birthing Center

Even if you don't choose a childbirth class sponsored by the facility at which you'll be giving birth, you should try to arrange a tour. On the tour, you can:

- Find out where you must park when you and your partner arrive at the center.
- Scope out the labor and birthing rooms.
- Get a feel for the staff's attitude and level of friendliness and approachability.
- Peek at the nursery and maternity ward.
- Observe newborn care.
- Acquaint yourself with hospital/center policy and procedures.

Milestones

Here is a place for you to record the thoughts, feelings, and physical changes you experience during your fifth month of pregnancy.

Time until due date: _____

Firsts:

....

....

....

Concerns:

....

....

....

Looking forward:

....

....

....

Questions for the doctor or midwife next month:

....

....

....

Journal

Date :   /   /

Journal

Date :   /   /

Journal

Date :   /   /

Journal

Date :   /   /

Journal

Date : / /

Part 7

Month Six

At six months, you may feel as though you'll be pregnant forever, but the final trimester will come and go before you know it. Take some time this month to savor pregnancy and treat yourself to some of the indulgences that only a mother-to-be can pull off.

Month Six Checklist

✓ Take a day off and pamper yourself.
✓ Start putting together your birth plan.
✓ Think about who you want in the delivery room.
✓ Begin listing baby names.

Your Baby This Month

Feeling a rhythmic lurch in your abdomen? Your little girl probably has the hiccups, a common phenomenon thought to be brought on by drinking and/or breathing amniotic fluid. They'll go away on their own, eventually.

The once-transparent skin of your baby is starting to thicken, and sweat glands are developing below the skin surface. She's over a foot long now, and by the end of the month she may weigh up to two pounds.

Your Body's Changes

Your uterus extends well above your navel now. You may actually be seeing fetal movement across your abdomen as your baby gets comfortable in her shrinking living space. You will also notice that your feet have begun to swell. This is a result of the dramatic increase in blood volume you've experienced, which is feeding excess fluids to surrounding tissues, resulting in edema (or water retention). To make matters worse, the weight of your uterus is requiring the veins in your legs to work double time to pump all that extra blood back to your heart. Estrogen also increases the amount of fluid your tissues absorb.

The result of all this is puffy and sometimes aching feet. Putting your feet up when you can, wearing comfortable low-heeled shoes, and soaking your feet in cool water are all good ways to ease the discomfort. Special compression stockings, available at medical supply stores, may also be helpful.

If you experience sudden and severe swelling of the face and hands, call your doctor or midwife immediately. It may be a sign of preeclampsia, also called toxemia, a condition that is potentially hazardous to both you and your baby. Other signs of preeclampsia include:

- High blood pressure
- Headaches
- Visual disturbances
- Sudden excessive weight gain
- Protein in the urine

Symptoms on the menu yet again this month include the following. Check off any that you are experiencing so that you can ask your doctor or midwife about them and to track the progress of your pregnancy:

___ Nausea
___ Fatigue
___ Frequent urination
___ Tender and/or swollen breasts

___ Bleeding gums

___ Excess mucus and saliva

___ Increase in vaginal discharge

___ Mild shortness of breath

___ Lightheadedness or dizziness

___ Headaches

___ Forgetfulness

___ Gas

___ Heartburn

___ Constipation

___ Skin and hair changes

___ Round ligament pain or soreness

___ Lower back aches

___ Mild swelling of legs, feet, and hands

___ Leg cramps

On Your Mind

As you sidle up to the third trimester starting line, try to take advantage of these final days of relative comfort and sit back and savor your pregnancy. Try each of these ways to pamper yourself:

- Splurge for a day spa treatment.
- Spend a lazy afternoon curled up with a good book.
- Cool off with a dish of your favorite Ben & Jerry's flavor.
- Enjoy a nice, relaxing soak in the tub.
- Take a scenic weekend drive with no deadlines or particular destination.
- Use the valet service to park instead of hiking from the lot.
- Order healthy carry-out fare from your favorite restaurant.

Prenatal Visit Notes

Stats

Weight
....

Week of pregnancy
....

Fundal height
....

Blood pressure
....

Baby's heart rate
....

Tests

Test	*Result*
....	....
....	....
....	....
....	....

Additional Notes

....

....

....

....

At the Doctor's or Midwife's Office

There will be more of the same this month as your provider checks your weight and fundal height, listens to your baby's heartbeat, and finds out about any new pregnancy symptoms you may be experiencing. Your doctor or midwife will also require the usual urine sample and blood pressure check.

If you weren't given an oral glucose tolerance test to screen for gestational diabetes last month, it will probably be administered now.

Birth Plan Checklist

Now is a good time to go through a birth plan checklist. A birth plan is a road map for your entire childbirth experience, beginning to end. It's your chance to let everyone involved (doctors, nurses, partners) know what you want the experience to be. Use your birth plan to chart the course of labor and delivery, but remember you may have to take alternate routes occasionally depending on conditions.

1. Where will the birth take place?
    ___ Hospital
    ___ Birthing center
    ___ Home
    ___ Other: _____

2.   Who will be there for labor support?

___ Husband or significant other
___ Doula
___ Friend
___ Family member

3.   Will any room modifications or equipment be required to increase your mental and physical comfort?

___ Objects from home, such as pictures and a blanket and pillow
___ Lighting adjustments
___ Music
___ Video or photos of birth
___ Other: _____

4.   Do you have any special requests for labor prep procedures?

___ Forgo enema
___ Self-administer the enema
___ Forgo shaving
___ Shave self
___ Heparin lock instead of routine IV line
___ Other: _____

5.   What do you want to eat and drink during labor?

___ A light snack
___ Water, sports drink, or other appropriate beverage
___ Ice chips
___ Other: _____

6. Do you want pain medication?

___ Analgesic, such as Stadol, Demerol, or Nubain
___ Epidural
___ Other: _____

7. What nonpharmaceutical pain relief equipment might you want access to?

___ Hydrotherapy, such as a shower or whirlpool
___ Warm compresses
___ Birth ball
___ Other: _____

8. What interventions would you like to avoid unless deemed a medical necessity by your provider during labor? Specify your preferred alternatives.

— Episiotomy
— Forceps
— Internal fetal monitoring
— Pitocin (oxytocin)
— Other: _____

9. What would you like your first face-to-face with your baby to be like?

— Hold off on all nonessential treatment, evaluation, and tests for a specified time.
— If immediate tests and evaluation is necessary, you, your partner, or another support person will accompany the baby.
— Want to nurse immediately following birth.
— Would like family members to meet the baby immediately following birth.
— Other: _____

10. If a Caesarean section is required, what is important to you and your partner?

— Type of anesthesia (e.g., general vs. spinal block)
— Having partner or another support person present

— Spending time with the baby immediately following procedure
— Bonding with the baby in the recovery room
— Type of postoperative pain relief and nursing considerations
— Other: _____

11. Do you have a preference for who cuts the cord?

— You
— Your partner
— Provider

12. When would you like the cut to be performed?

— Delay until cord stops pulsing.
— Cord blood will be banked. Cut per banking guidelines.
— Cut at provider's discretion.
— Other: _____

13. What kind of postpartum care will you and the baby have at the hospital?

— Baby will room-in with mom.
— Baby will sleep in the nursery at night.
— Baby will breastfeed.
— Baby will bottle feed.
— Baby will not be fed any supplemental formula and/or glucose water unless medically indicated.
— Baby will not be given a pacifier.
— Other: _____

14. What are your considerations for after discharge?

— Support and short-term care for siblings
— Support if you've had a Caesarean
— Maternity leave
— Other: _____

Thinking of Names

You and your significant other have no doubt been thinking about the potential name you will choose depending on the gender of the baby. To get you started on ideas, below are the most popular names for babies born in 2005.

Boys' Names	Girls' Names
Jacob	Emily
Michael	Emma
Joshua	Madison
Matthew	Abigail
Ethan	Olivia
Andrew	Isabella
Daniel	Hanna
Anthony	Samantha
Christopher	Ava
Joseph	Ashley

Source: U.S. Social Security Administration

Here you can record boys' names that you and your partner like.

....

....

....

....

....

....

....

....

....

....

....

....

....

....

....

....

Here you can record girls' names that you and your partner like.

....

....

....

....

....

....

....

....

....

....

....

....

....

....

....

....

....

....

Milestones

Here is a place for you to record the thoughts, feelings, and physical changes you experience during your sixth month of pregnancy.

Time until due date: _____

Firsts:

....

....

....

Concerns:

....

....

....

Looking forward:

....

....

....

Questions for the doctor or midwife next month:

....

....

....

Journal

Date : / /

Journal

Date :   /   /

Journal

Date : / /

Journal

Date :   /   /

Journal

Date : / /

Part 8

Month Seven

You're likely feeling perpetually stuffed and slightly out of breath as your uterus relocates all your internal organs. The relief and energy felt in the second trimester may start to fade now. Just remember, you're almost there!

Month Seven Checklist

✓ Make a date with yourself to relax, read, or just catch up on sleep.
✓ Interview pediatricians.
✓ Sign up for childbirth classes.
✓ Contemplate the breast versus bottle decision.
✓ Set up an appointment to discuss your birth plan with your provider.

Your Baby This Month

Weighing in at four pounds and about sixteen inches long, your baby is growing amazingly fast now. His red, wrinkled skin is losing its fine lanugo covering as more insulating fat accumulates. And his eyelids, closed for so long, can now open and afford him a dim view of the place he will call home for just a few more months.

Dramatic developments in the brain and central nervous system are also occurring. Your baby feels pain, can cry, and responds to stimulation from light or sound outside the womb. Periodically, tiny elbows and feet will turn your belly into an interactive relief map.

Your Body's Changes

The top of the fundus is halfway between your belly button and your breastbone, displacing your stomach, intestines, and diaphragm.

Your breasts are heavier and more glandular and are getting ready to feed your baby. In this last trimester, your nipples may begin to leak colostrum, which is the yellowish, nutrient-rich fluid that precedes real breast milk. To reduce backaches and breast tenderness, make sure you wear a well-fitting bra (even to bed if it helps). If you are planning on breastfeeding, you may want to start buying the following few things now that can take you through the rest of pregnancy and right into the postpartum period in preparation for nursing:

- **Nursing bra:** Try out the clasps for easy nursing access. Try to unfasten and slip the nursing flaps down with one hand.
- **Sports bra:** Instead of a nursing bra, you may opt for the comfort of a sports bra that slides up easily.
- **Easy-access shirts:** Button-up blouses, shirts with zippers, and other easy-access clothing will make nursing easier on a day-to-day basis.
- **Nursing pads:** These pads, which catch leaks before they soak through your shirt, come in several different materials and configurations, including cloth, plastic, and disposable.

If you will not be breastfeeding but using formula or bottle-feeding breast milk instead, look for a bottle with these characteristics:

- **Low air flow:** Designs that minimize air or can be de-aired prior to feeding may reduce your baby's gas.
- **Convenience:** If saving time is a priority, features like presterilized disposable bag bottles are a big plus.
- **Easy to clean:** Pick something with minimal parts that looks relatively easy to clean and sterilize.
- **Built for baby:** Make sure your baby gets a newborn-style nipple with a smaller opening to start so he doesn't face a formula tidal wave. If his sucking reflex is weak, however, you may have to upgrade to a larger opening.

Your body is warming up for labor, and you may start to experience Braxton Hicks contractions. These painless and irregular contractions feel as if your uterus is making a fist and then gradually relaxing it. If your little one is fairly active, you may think that he is stretching himself sideways at first. A quick check of your belly may reveal a visible tightening.

Braxton Hicks can begin as early as week twenty and continue right up until your due date, although they're more commonly felt in the final month of pregnancy.

The list is growing. Other symptoms that may continue this month include:

___ Fatigue
___ Frequent urination
___ Tender and/or swollen breasts
___ Bleeding gums
___ Excess mucus and saliva
___ Increase in vaginal discharge
___ Mild shortness of breath
___ Lightheadedness or dizziness
___ Headaches
___ Forgetfulness
___ Gas
___ Heartburn
___ Constipation
___ Skin and hair changes
___ Round ligament pain or soreness
___ Lower back aches
___ Mild swelling of legs, feet, and hands
___ Leg cramps

On Your Mind

As labor looms closer your thoughts turn to the task at hand. Going into labor and delivery with as much knowledge of the process as possible can make the difference between a positive childbirth experience and a long and arduous one. You may now be wondering whether you are up to the task of labor and whether you will be up to the task of motherhood.

Remember that women have been doing this since the beginning of time, and under much more difficult circumstances. In most cases labor will be hard work, but if you prepare yourself by learning what to expect, you will be ready to face whatever comes your way.

Also keep in mind that great moms are made, not born. While some parts of mothering will seem to come to you instinctively, practice and trial and error will make up the better part of your parenting education. Use the tools around you—your pediatrician, other mothers, and research and reading—to build and sharpen your skills, but listen to your inner voice in the final analysis and application of what you learn.

At the Doctor's or Midwife's Office

Starting with this initial third-trimester visit, your visits to the doctor may start to step up to twice monthly. Women who are Rh negative will need treatment with Rh immune globulin (RhoGAM) this month. An injection is typically given at about twenty-eight weeks to protect the fetus from developing hemolytic disease—a condition in which the mother's antibodies attack the fetal red blood cells.

Stats

Weight
....

Week of pregnancy
....

Fundal height
....

Blood pressure
....

Baby's heart rate
....

Tests

Test	*Result*
....	....
....	....
....	....
....	....

Additional Notes

....

....

....

....

Choosing a Pediatrician

Your pediatrician will look in on and care for your newborn in the hospital, so getting one lined up now is important. Some things to inquire about beyond the basic office hours and insurance questions include:

Do ill children have a waiting room separate from the one for well-child visits?

....

....

Will the doctor support your feeding choice?

....

....

Are lactation consultants available?

....

....

How are calls into the office triaged and returned?

....

....

Additional questions or concerns:

....

....

Arranging Child Care

Now is also a good time to begin scoping out potential child care providers. Your best source of leads for good child care is other moms in your life who share your values and viewpoints on child rearing. Then narrow down your list of facilities based on the answers to the following questions. You should visit and observe children at any facility you are considering for your own child.

1. Does the facility have adequate staffing? (For infants, this is generally a minimum of one provider to every three babies.)

   ....

   ....

   ....

   ....

   ....

2. Does the facility provide a stimulating and child-friendly environment?

   ....

   ....

   ....

   ....

   ....

3. What is the staff like? (Are they caring and nurturing, or do they seem to be distracted or overburdened?)

....

....

....

....

4. Is the facility properly licensed and accredited? (See the Web site of the National Association for the Education of Young Children, *www .naeyc.org*, if you are unsure.)

....

....

....

....

5. Is an adequate number of the staff specially trained for early childhood care?

....

....

....

....

6. Do the children in the program seem comfortable and happy?

....

....

....

7. Are parents allowed to observe when their child is in the program?

....

....

....

8. Does the program focus on emotional, cognitive, and physical development in activities?

....

....

....

9. Does the staff provide adequate individual attention to infants?

....

....

....

....

Milestones

Here is a place for you to record the thoughts, feelings, and physical changes you experience during your seventh month of pregnancy.

Time until due date: _____

Firsts:

....

....

....

Concerns:

....

....

....

Looking forward:

....

....

....

Questions for the doctor or midwife next month:

....

....

....

Journal

Date :   /   /

Journal

Date : / /

Journal

Date : / /

Journal

Date :   /   /

Journal

Date : / /

Part 9

Month Eight

You are a pregnancy pro now, deftly handling all the aches and pains that come with the territory. You've learned to adjust to the fashion hardships, the lifestyle changes, and the logistical challenges that your baby and belly have brought to the forefront. It's not much longer now.

Month Eight Checklist

✓ Take five and de-stress; it's good for you and baby.
✓ Lay out your baby's essentials.
✓ Compare and decide on cloth versus disposal diapers.
✓ Discuss circumcision with your pediatrician and your partner.
✓ Start wrapping up projects at work.
✓ Finalize your child care plans for after maternity leave.
✓ Preregister at your hospital or birthing center.

Your Baby This Month

Gradually shifting to the same position in which 95 percent of all babies are born, your baby starts to move into a head down pose, known as the vertex position.

Your little one is now up to eighteen inches long and as heavy as a five-pound sack of flour. The rest of her body is finally catching up to the size of her head. Although it may feel like your baby is constantly up and about, she's actually sleeping 90 to 95 percent of the day, a figure that will drop only slightly when she is born.

If your child were born today, she'd have an excellent chance of surviving and eventually thriving outside the womb. However, she'd still be considered preterm or premature, just as any birth before thirty-seven weeks of gestation.

Your Body's Changes

Weight gain should start to slow down this month. If it doesn't, however, don't cut your calorie intake below 2,600 to try and stop it. You need the extra energy for both of you.

As your baby settles firmly on your bladder, bathroom stops step up once again. You may even experience some stress incontinence, which is minor dribbling or leakage of urine when you sneeze, cough, laugh, or make other sudden movements. This should clear up postpartum.

Other symptoms that may begin or continue this month include:

__ Fatigue

__ Frequent urination

__ Tender and/or swollen breasts

__ Colostrum discharge from nipples

__ Bleeding gums

__ Excess mucus and saliva

__ Increase in vaginal discharge

__ Mild shortness of breath

__ Lightheadedness or dizziness

__ Headaches

__ Forgetfulness

__ Gas

__ Heartburn

__ Constipation

__ Skin and hair changes

__ Round ligament pain or soreness

__ Lower back aches

__ Mild swelling of legs, feet, and hands

__ Leg cramps

___ Painless, irregular Braxton Hicks contractions
___ Minor vision changes (fluid retention can slightly change the shape of your eyes and estrogen can cause your eyes to be drier than normal)

On Your Mind

As labor looms closer, your thoughts turn to the task at hand. Going into labor and delivery with as much knowledge of the process as possible can make the difference between a positive childbirth experience and a long and arduous one, so continue to read and ask questions.

At the Doctor's or Midwife's Office

You'll see your provider twice this month as you continue your every-other-week routine. He or she will check the position of your baby to determine if she has turned head down in preparation for birth.

Prenatal Visit Notes

Stats

Weight

....

Week of pregnancy

....

Fundal height

....

Blood pressure

....

Baby's heart rate

....

Tests

Test   *Result*

....

....

....

....

Additional Notes

....

....

....

....

Nesting

At this time you will probably be feeling the urge to make your home as cozy and welcoming for your baby as possible. Here are some baby essentials you should have on the shelves prior to her arrival:

___ Diapers
___ Wipes
___ Alcohol swabs (for her umbilical cord)
___ Baby shampoo
___ Baby soap
___ Diaper rash ointment
___ Waterproof pads (for cutting down on laundry)
___ Bottles (even if you're breastfeeding you may pump milk occasionally)
___ Thermometer
___ Infant Tylenol or another fever-reducing product as recommended by your pediatrician
___ Baby blankets

The Diaper Debate

Deciding whether you'd like to use cloth diapers or disposable diapers is a choice many new mothers go back and forth on. Some moms swear by the old-fashioned and eco-friendly use of cloth diapers, while others find the convenience of disposable diapers a necessity. Your decision may depend on a variety of factors, including your concern about the environment, the amount of time and labor you are willing to devote to maintaining a supply of clean diapers, and the level of convenience that would work best for you from day to day.

Below you will find a list of pros and cons to help you decide where you stand in the cloth versus disposable diaper debate.

Using Cloth Diapers

Pros

Biodegradable
Cheaper than plastic
Can be less irritating for baby's skin

Cons

Requires electricity and water to wash
Can become expensive if you hire a service to wash diapers
Labor intensive if you wash them yourself

Call local diaper services to get estimates and a run-down of what's included.

Cloth Diaper Service Research

Service name
....

Phone number
....

Address
....

....

Cost per week
....

Services included for cost
....

....

Service name
....

Phone number
....

Address
....

....

Cost per week
....

Services included for cost
....

....

Service name
....

Phone number
....

Address
....

....

Cost per week
....

Services included for cost
....

....

Service name
....

Phone number
....

Address
....

....

Cost per week
....

Services included for cost
....

....

Service name
....

Phone number
....

Address
....

....

Cost per week
....

Services included for cost
....

....

Service name
....

Phone number
....

Address
....

....

Cost per week
....

Services included for cost
....

....

Planning for the postpartum period can be a tremendous help in getting organized after you and your baby are back at home.

Will you have live-in help (other than that from your partner) for a few days or weeks?

....

Helper Contact Info

Helper's name:
....

Helper's phone number:
....

Helper's e-mail address:
....

Helper's address:
....

....

Dates and times available to help:

....

....

Have you arranged childcare for the baby's siblings?

....

....

....

Caretaker Contact Info

Caretaker's name:
....

Caretaker's phone number:
....

Caretaker's e-mail address:
....

Caretaker's address:
....

Dates and times available to watch siblings:

....

....

Scheduled Time Off

Are you and your partner both taking time off?

....

Dates of your time off:

....

....

....

Dates of your partner's time off:

....

....

....

Will your baby have a whirlwind schedule of introductions to friends and family, or just a few exclusive engagements?

....

....

....

....

....

....

....

....

....

....

....

....

....

....

....

....

....

After running your postpartum plans by your healthcare provider, record any special discharge instructions from your doctor for you or your baby.

....

....

....

....

....

....

....

....

....

....

....

....

....

....

....

....

....

Milestones

Here is a place for you to record the thoughts, feelings, and physical changes you experience during your eighth month of pregnancy.

Time until due date: _____

Firsts:

....

....

....

Concerns:

....

....

....

Looking forward:

....

....

....

Questions for the doctor or midwife next month:

....

....

....

Journal

Date: /   /

Journal

Date: / /

Journal

Date: /   /

Journal

Date :   /   /

Journal

Date :   /   /

Part 10

Month Nine

The grand finale is approaching. You may feel like you've been waiting forever. But even if you had the time of conception pinpointed, your baby may decide he needs a little more, or a little less, time preparing. Never fear; he will arrive sooner or later.

Month Nine Checklist

✓ Make sure that your other children's teachers and care providers are aware of your impending hospital stay.
✓ Pack your bag and compile a call list for your partner.
✓ Line up postpartum assistance.
✓ Stock up the freezer with heat-and-eat meals or recruit postpartum kitchen help.
✓ Make a plan, and a back-up plan, for getting to the hospital.
✓ Put your feet up, relax, and take a deep breath. The rest is up to your baby!

Your Baby This Month

Your child is packing on about a half-pound per week as he prepares to make his big exit. He's fully formed and just waiting for the right time now. His lungs, the last organ system to fully mature, now have an adequate level of surfactant in them to allow for breathing outside of the womb.

Your Body's Changes

While your baby is still growing, your weight gain tapers off, and you may even lose a pound or so due to a drop in amniotic fluid production. Many more things are happening this month. Check off those you experience, note when they occur, and call your doctor or midwife with any questions.

___ Groin soreness
___ Backache
___ As your cervix thins and dilates (opens), the soft mucous plug keeping it sealed tight may be dislodged
___ Increased need to urinate
___ Feel shockwaves through your pelvis as your baby settles further down onto the pelvic floor

Braxton Hicks contractions may be more frequent this month as you draw nearer to delivery. You're close enough to be on the lookout for the real thing, however. You know you are experiencing real contractions when they:

• Are felt in the back and possibly radiate around to the abdomen.
• Do not subside when you move around or change positions.
• Increase in intensity with activity like walking.
• Increase in intensity as time passes.
• Come at roughly regular intervals (early on this may be from twenty to forty-five minutes apart).

Other signs that labor is on its way include amniotic fluid leaks in either a gush or a trickle (your water breaking), sudden diarrhea, and the appearance of the mucous plug. For many women, the bag of waters does not break until active labor sets in.

On Your Mind

You're likely tired but happy as you pack and prepare for the big day. Just remember the "estimated" in estimated delivery date to avoid a big letdown if baby is tardy.

As sleep gets more and more elusive and your discomfort increases, you may find yourself easily provoked. To keep your cool and limit anxiety:

- Stay clear of encounters with people you know will irritate you.
- Ask your significant other to be the point person on all "anything yet?" questions.
- Take a deep breath and go over what you learned in childbirth class.
- Talk with your partner or labor coach about ways to relax.
- Ask your provider any questions that may still be on your mind about labor and delivery.

At the Doctor's or Midwife's Office

You'll see your doctor or midwife on a weekly basis now until you deliver. You should expect that your provider will:

- Perform an internal exam with each visit to check your cervix for changes that indicate approaching labor.
- Administer a group B strep (GBS) test one month prior to your estimated delivery date.
- Take note of any descent or dropping of the baby toward the pelvis. This descent is called the pelvic station.

Stats

Weight
....

Week of pregnancy
....

Fundal height
....

Blood pressure
....

Baby's heart rate
....

Tests

Test   *Result*

....

....

....

....

Additional Notes

....

....

....

....

Gearing Up for the Big Event

Since a baby's timetable is somewhat unpredictable, start getting your affairs in order at the beginning of this month. Make sure to:

__ Double-check with your doctor or midwife that a copy of your birth plan has been put into your chart.

__ See that your birth plan includes any changes you might have made to it since your first review together.

__ Provide your labor coach with an extra copy of your birth plan just in case the original is misplaced.

__ Take up friends, family, and neighbors on their offers of assistance. Make a list and schedule assignments (see the following chart on page 179 to compile this list).

__ Give friends who are good in the kitchen cooking detail, so you can have a supply of frozen, home-cooked meals on hand for easy dinners.

__ If you have other children, charge your husband or partner with making sure their school, extracurricular, and social schedules are covered.

__ Sound out the idea with your partner of asking a mommy-expert, maybe even your own mom, to come for a visit.

When family and friends offer to help you after the baby is born, first make sure they are making genuine offers. If they really do intend to help, take them up on their kindness! Allow these goodhearted people to take pets for walks, pick up groceries, or, if you have other children, to help you look after them. To keep track of the offers of family and friends to help you and your partner out postpartum, use this space to record the details.

Task	Individual Volunteering	Times Available to Help
....	....	....
....	....	....
....	....	....
....	....	....
....	....	....
....	....	....
....	....	....
....	....	....
....	....	....

Packing Your Bag

Essentials you should pack for your delivery include:

Pain-relief tools for labor: Include things like massage balls, a picture for focusing on through contractions, a water bottle, and so forth.

Music to labor by: Check with your hospital or birthing center in advance to see if a small portable stereo is acceptable. If not, you can always bring personal headphones.

Snacks for the coach: Make sure it's something that won't turn your stomach if you see or smell it during labor.

Stopwatch, clock, or watch with a second hand: This will come in handy for timing contractions.

Camera: For capturing baby's arrival (or the moments shortly thereafter), don't forget the batteries and film (or an extra memory card)!

Phone numbers: Make sure your partner has names and numbers of the folks you'll want to clue in immediately on the new arrival.

Several nightgowns: Bring some with button or snap fronts if you're going to nurse.

Extra underwear: Make them comfortable but not your best. They'll probably end up with some postpartum bloodstains.

Sanitary pads: The hospital will provide you with some, but extras are good to have on hand.

Picture of the kids: If you have other children, taping a picture of big brother or sister to your newborn's bassinet is a good way to emphasize your first child's important new role in the family.

Glasses or contacts: Make sure you can see the baby after he's finally here.

Warm socks and/or slippers: Those hospital floors can be cold.

Bathrobe: You'll want this for hallway walks to the nursery.

Toiletries: Remember toothbrush, toothpaste, and other basics.

Shower supplies: You'll be given an opportunity to shower at the hospital, so pack shampoo and other necessities.

Going-home outfits for both you and your baby: Pack a set of newborn clothes and make sure you bring something loose and comfortable to wear yourself.

Baby blanket: You'll want to swaddle your baby for his return home. Let your partner bring the car seat on discharge day so you aren't overwhelmed with luggage.

If you're breastfeeding, you might also pack:

Nursing bras: If you don't have any yet, a bra with a front fastener will work well as a stand-in for now.

Box of nursing pads: These will be handy for when your milk comes in.

Vitamin E oil or lanolin ointment: Pack them for sore or cracked nipples.

Additional Items to Bring:

....

....

....

....

....

....

....

....

....

....

Outfitting Your Baby

In addition to some of the other products you may have purchased in anticipation of baby's arrival (diapers, wipes, car seat, alcohol swabs, baby shampoo, baby soap, bottles, and a thermometer), make sure you have the following before you bring your new baby home:

___ Three undershirts that snap
___ Ten onesies and/or one-piece sleepers
(depending on the season and climate you live in)
___ Five bibs with waterproof linings (e.g. rubber)
___ Three hooded bath towels
___ Seven pairs of booties or socks
___ Ten+ towels or cloth diapers for dealing with spit up
___ Four+ snap-up jumpsuits for daywear
___ Two+ baby hats
___ Nightlight
___ Baby monitor
___ Four+ crib or bassinet sheets
___ Four+ receiving blankets
___ Baby nail clippers
___ Four+ face cloths
___ Q-tips and/or cotton balls
___ Baby oil
___ Diaper rash ointment
___ Changing pad
___ Baby-strength sunscreen (SPF of 50 or higher;
check with your doctor about what is right for your child)

Items for Leaving the House

Once you and your baby are home from the hospital, you'll need a few items so that you can pay visits to friends and family (and be out and about) with everything you'll need to keep you and your baby comfortable. Some items you might consider purchasing are:

- Stroller
- Jogging stroller
- Diaper bag
- Backpack or convertible backpack/frontpack
- Carseat
- Toy for carseat
- Sling
- Sunshade

Additional Items to Buy:

....

....

....

....

....

....

....

....

Alerting Family and Friends

Here you can record the contact information for those people your partner or labor coach should call immediately when your baby is born to share the good news.

Person's Name	Phone Number	E-mail Address	Successfully Contacted?
....	....	....	....
....	....	....	....
....	....	....	....
....	....	....	....
....	....	....	....
....	....	....	....
....	....	....	....
....	....	....	....
....	....	....	....
....	....	....	....
....	....	....	....
....	....	....	....
....	....	....	....
....	....	....	....

Birth Announcement Contact Sheet

Record the contact information for anyone you want to send a birth announcement to.

Name:
....

Phone number:
....

E-mail address:
....

Address:
....

....

Name:
....

Phone number:
....

E-mail address:
....

Address:
....

....

Name:
....

Phone number:
....

E-mail address:
....

Address:
....

....

Name:
....

Phone number:
....

E-mail address:
....

Address:
....

....

Name:
....

Phone number:
....

E-mail address:
....

Address:
....

....

Name:
....

Phone number:
....

E-mail address:
....

Address:
....

....

....

Name:
....

Phone number:
....

E-mail address:
....

Address:
....

....

Name:
....

Phone number:
....

E-mail address:
....

Address:
....

....

Name:
....

Phone number:
....

E-mail address:
....

Address:
....

....

Labor Time Checklist for Your Partner

Remembering everything in the thrill of the big moment may be hard, so make a checklist and keep it on your car's dashboard so that you remember everything when the time comes. Also remember to top off your gas tank every time it gets below the halfway mark, so that you won't have to make a stop for gas on the way to the hospital.

Overnight bag ○

Cell phone, calling card, or plenty of quarters for pay-phone calls
(if cell phones are not allowed to be used in the hospital) ○

Phone number list (see page 184) ○

○

○

○

○

○

○

○

○

○

○

○

○

○

○

○

○

○

○

○

Baby Gifts

Be sure to record the sender and gift item for all baby gifts you receive. That way you will have an easy reference for when you are well-rested and ready to send out thank you cards!

Gift Item	Sender	Date Card Mailed
....	....	....
....	....	....
....	....	....
....	....	....
....	....	....
....	....	....
....	....	....
....	....	....
....	....	....
....	....	....
....	....	....
....	....	....
....	....	....
....	....	....
....	....	....

Gift Item	Sender	Date Card Mailed

Gift Item	Sender	Date Card Mailed

Labor and Delivery

Time of first contraction:
....

Where you were when labor began:
....

Date admitted:
....

Time admitted:
....

Delivery date:
....

Delivery time:
....

Baby's length:
....

Baby's weight:
....

Any complications during labor and delivery:
....

....

....

Additional information about delivery:
....

....

....

....

....

....

....

....

Milestones

Here is a place for you to record the thoughts, feelings, and physical changes you experience during your ninth month of pregnancy.

Time until due date: _____

Firsts:

....

....

....

Concerns:

....

....

....

Looking forward:

....

....

....

Questions for the doctor or midwife:

....

....

....

Journal

Date :   /   /

Journal

Date :   /   /

Journal

Date: /   /

Journal

Date: /   /

Journal

Date :   /   /

The Postpartum Period

Part 11

Bringing Baby Home

The first days at home with your new family are fun but challenging. Your body is going through some intense physical changes. Enjoy this special time getting acquainted and settling into your new lifestyle.

Your Body Postpartum

From the moment your child slides out of your body, a transformation as dramatic as that of pregnancy begins. Right at delivery you will drop around 10 to 15 pounds of baby, placenta, amniotic fluid, and lochia.

By the tenth day postpartum, your uterus will have contracted to one-twentieth of its prelabor size and the cervix will be closed once again. Afterpains similar to menstrual cramps and a steady discharge of lochia indicate that the uterus is returning to normal. The lochia flow will continue up to 6 weeks, but the afterpains will probably stop several days after delivery (although nursing may continue to stimulate them periodically). Your perineal area may continue to be sore for a few weeks. Some things you can use to ease pain and swelling are:

- A hot water bottle
- The peribottle you may have received at the hospital
- Occasional cold packs
- A foam "donut" from a medical supply store for your chair (if sitting is uncomfortable)

As your body drops tissue, fluids, and decreases its cardiovascular volume, your metabolism may seem out of whack. In addition, you may find the following:

- Vaginally, things may seem a little "looser." Vaginal skin is elastic, and may be stretched out from the birth. Exercise and time will help it return to a firmer state.
- Constipation is another common postpartum problem. Plenty of water, movement, and high-fiber foods may help.
- Your breasts will be tender as you deal with engorgement. If you breastfeed, sore nipples and other discomforts may be plaguing you as you adjust to this new routine.

Recovering after Caesarean

When you've had a C-section you're recovering from major surgery and need to treat yourself accordingly.

- Sleep when baby sleeps and stay away from strenuous activity and heavy lifting (nothing bigger than baby as a general rule).
- Use a bed pillow or a nursing pillow to hold your baby without pressuring your incision.
- Pain medication may be prescribed; if you're breastfeeding, talk to your doctor about judicious use.
- Your doctor will recommend 6 weeks of rest and recuperation and you'll be advised not to drive while taking pain medications.
- Above all, don't push it, or you'll set your recovery back even further.

Your Baby's Body

Your baby will actually lose weight as she starts out in life, but should be back up to birth weight by her 2-week checkup. Thereafter, she may put on 1 pound every 2 weeks, doubling her birth weight by month 4. Premature babies sometimes grow a little slower, but most will eventually catch up.

Reflexes

Your newborn arrives with a variety of natural reflexes or involuntary ways of moving:

- **Palmar, or grasping, reflex.** When you touch your baby's open hand, she'll make a fist around your finger.
- **Rooting reflex.** If you stroke her cheek, her head will turn toward your touch. This reflex helps your newborn find her food source.
- **Sucking reflex.** Once at the breast or bottle, your baby's sucking reflex takes over as she automatically sucks on anything put in her mouth.
- **Startle, or moro, reflex.** When your baby is startled, he will thrust his arms and legs out and arch his back, then quickly pull arms and legs in again.
- **Babinski reflex.** Stroking your baby's foot will make him spread his toes and flex his foot in.
- **Stepping reflex.** If you hold your baby up with your hands under her armpits so that her feet are touching a firm surface, she will lift her feet up and down.
- **Tonic neck reflex.** When placed on his back, baby turns his head to the right and makes fists with his hands.
- **Blinking.** The involuntary reflex of closing her eyes when they are exposed to bright light, air, or another stimulus is the one reflex that your baby will keep for the rest of her life.

Birthmarks

Your baby may be born with one or more birthmarks.

- **Red marks on the eyelids**, forehead, and at the very back of the nape of the neck usually fade and disappear over time and are called salmon patches or stork bites.
- **Red, strawberry birthmarks** can increase in size but may shrink and be gone by age five.
- **Very rarely, light brown birthmarks known as café au lait spots** (particularly a large number) are symptomatic of medical conditions. Talk to your child's doctor if you have any concerns.
- **Dark blue to blue-green spots** on the buttocks or lower back are known as Mongolian spots, which are most common in African-American, Native American, and Asian newborns and fade over time.
- **For port wine stains**, bright red or purple marks that are considered to be more permanent, plastic surgery is an option in later life if they are located in a prominent spot.
- **Little whiteheads called milia** are common on newborns, especially around the nose, and may come and go during the first few days.
- **Petechia are red to purple pinpoints** that you may see on your baby's face from the trauma of coming down the birth canal. These will disappear in a few days.

The Umbilical Cord

Baby's umbilical cord stump looks like a dark, dried up protrusion. You'll be instructed to:

- Clean it regularly, usually with alcohol swabs
- Keep it dry to prevent breakage and bleeding
- Keep an eye open for signs of infection, such as pus or inflammation

Within 2 weeks or so, the stump will fall off and your baby's perfect little belly button will be revealed.

Breast or Bottle?

Are you going to breastfeed or go the formula route? If you were comparing breast milk to formula strictly on a nutrient basis, few would disagree that the best choice is breast milk. But since the issue is also loaded with social, emotional, and personal considerations, things are seldom so black and white. In the end, breast or bottle is an individual choice.

Your Body and Breastfeeding

In the first few days following birth, your breasts will produce a clear to yellow sticky substance called colostrum. Colostrum contains antibodies that help strengthen the infant immune system. It also is important for getting baby's digestion off on the right track. The low-carbohydrate, high-protein concoction is easily digestible for these early days and helps to establish beneficial bacteria in your baby's gastrointestinal tract.

Colostrum comes out in small amounts compared to later breast milk. You'll know when your milk "comes in" because your breasts will become:

- Engorged with milk
- Very hard
- Sore to the touch

Nursing your baby will relieve some of the pressure quickly, although it's possible you may need a little additional help to ease soreness.

Ways to relieve soreness include the following.

- Cold compresses between feedings
- Warm compresses
- Gentle breast massage
- Refrigerated cabbage leaves, draped over the breast, inside bra
- Warm showers

Breastfeeding Pros and Cons

PRO: Breast milk is custom made for your child's nutritional needs and provides essential antibodies.
CON: If you have a medical condition that requires drug treatment, it's possible your medication may pass into breast milk.

PRO: Breastfeeding is a low-maintenance feeding routine. Never needs mixing, warming, or other preparation.
CON: You will always need to be close at hand. Breastfeeding can be physically taxing.

PRO: Nursing gives you special one-on-one bonding time with baby.
CON: No one else can pitch in on the feeding duties.

PRO: Breastfeeding is a big cost-cutter. Aside from the high cost of formula, you can save on bottles, bags, and other formula feeding purchases.
CON: You may have to purchase or rent a breast pump and buy a personal kit to use with it, which can be costly.

PRO: Many women who breastfeed experience faster postpartum weight loss.
CON: Although you may be taking your figure back, your breasts belong to baby—leaks, sore nipples, and all.

Notes about breastfeeding:

....

....

....

....

....

....

....

Bottle Feeding Pros and Cons

PRO: Feeding isn't only mom, all day and all night.
CON: The special mother-child bond and skin-to-skin contact that breastfeeding brings may be harder to achieve.

PRO: You can give your baby a bottle just about anywhere, anytime without feeling self-conscious or raising eyebrows.
CON: Make sure you pack sterilized bottles and nipples, formula, bottled water for mixing, a can opener for opening premixed formula, and more.

PRO: No worries about keeping up your milk supply when you return to work.
CON: You may miss out on a golden opportunity to spend special nursing time together at home once your work schedule starts.

PRO: You can assume control of your body again.

CON: After so many months as one, you're suddenly severing a close physical bond that nursing can prolong.

Notes about bottle feeding:

....

....

....

....

....

....

....

With all nursing positions, make sure your baby's head is well supported. After you're settled into position, brace your breast with one hand, cupped into the shape of a "C." Encouraging baby to get a successful latch is the most important part of the process. Stroke her bottom lip with your nipple until she opens her mouth wide and yawn-like. This is called the rooting reflex. Insert your nipple into her mouth and she should instinctively close, or latch, onto it. A proper latch:

- Encompasses the entire nipple and most, if not all, of the areola
- Positions her nose almost directly on your breast
- Can be verified by her visible and possibly audible swallowing
- Will not hurt (unless the nipple is in poor condition to begin with)

Postpartum Depression

Feeling down is a common postpartum emotion that typically passes in a few weeks. For many women, however, these feelings go beyond the basic baby blues and signal a more serious depressive or endocrine disorder.

The Baby Blues

The majority of new mothers experience what has become known as "the baby blues," a short-lived period of mild depression that appears in up to 85 percent of postpartum women. A severe shortage of sleep, disappointment with the birth experience, fluctuating hormone levels, anxieties about your baby's health and well-being, and shaky confidence in your own parenting skills can all lead to feelings of sadness and inadequacy. Fortunately, most cases of the blues resolve themselves within a few days to 2 weeks after birth as balance returns to the new mother's life.

More Than the Blues

Postpartum depression (PPD) occurs in about 10 percent of new mothers, and can drag on for up to a year. Check off any of the following symptoms if you are experiencing them and talk to your doctor about PPD:

___ Feelings of extreme sadness and inexplicable crying jags
___ Lack of pleasure in things you would normally enjoy
___ Trouble concentrating
___ Excessive worrying about the baby, or conversely, a lack of interest in the baby
___ Feelings of low self-esteem
___ Decreased appetite

___ Feelings of resentment

___ Feelings of isolation

Fortunately, PPD can be effectively treated with counseling and/or antidepressant drugs, so ask your doctor for a referral to a mental health professional.

Thyroid Problems

Thyroid problems are fairly common after childbirth, but the symptoms can be confused with other postpartum conditions. Note whether you experience any of the following common signs of postpartum thyroid conditions and contact your doctor.

___ Milk supply difficulties

___ Extreme fatigue

___ Hair loss

___ Depression

___ Mood changes

___ Problems losing weight

___ Unusually rapid weight loss

___ Heart palpitations

___ Menstrual irregularities

___ Sleep disorders

Some women have temporary postpartum hyperthyroidism— an overactive thyroid, with weight loss, diarrhea, racing heart, anxiety, and other symptoms of a revved up metabolism. Doctors may prescribe drugs to ease symptoms, but this condition often resolves itself quickly. Other women can develop temporary postpartum hypothyroidism—an underactive thyroid—with fatigue, weight gain, constipation, depression, and other symptoms of a sloweddown metabolism. Again, medication may be prescribed, depending on the severity of symptoms, and frequently the thyroid will return to normal within 6 months to a year after the birth.

Don't Forget to Have Fun

Once you get past the fatigue, the uncertainties, and the occasional frustrations, being a new mom can be incredibly entertaining. You have a legitimate excuse to play, explore, rhyme, sing, and revisit your childhood in general. You have an adoring little person who hangs on your every word and movement and loves you unconditionally. And you get to witness all her incredible firsts as your baby learns to smile, roll over, crawl, and eventually walk and talk. In a year, this postpartum time will be a distant memory. Treasure it while it's here.

Postpartum Doctor's Visit

Here you can record any questions you may have for your doctor about the postpartum period, or any concerns you may wish to discuss with your provider.

....

....

....

....

....

....

....

....

....

....

....

....

....

....

....

Journal

Date :   /   /

Journal

Date :   /   /

Journal

Date :   /   /

Journal

Date :   /   /

Journal

Date: /   /

Appendix A

Frequently Asked
Questions

Will the bottle of champagne I shared with my husband on the night we conceived our baby be harmful?
Put this night of celebration behind you and stop feeling guilty. Binge drinking or regular abuse of alcohol when you are pregnant can cause birth defects, but an isolated episode of too much champagne probably has not harmed your unborn baby.

Heavy drinking, including binges or daily use, is especially associated with congenital defects. Babies born with fetal alcohol syndrome (FAS) show retarded growth, have central nervous system problems, and characteristic facial features, including a small head, a thin upper lip, a short upturned nose, a flattened nasal bridge and a general underdeveloped look of the face. Because of the critical nervous system involvement, many show tremulousness, can't suck, are hyperactive, have abnormal muscle tone, and are later diagnosed with attention deficit disorder as well as mental retardation.

Relying on alcohol out of habit or cravings can also end your pregnancy abruptly. Heavy to moderate drinkers seem to experience a higher incidence of miscarriage in the second trimester, as well as problems with the placenta. Other complications linked to alcohol use are congenital heart defects, brain abnormalities, spinal and limb defects, and urinary and genital problems.

What should I take for a headache?
Most doctors say that aspirin is fine for most of your pregnancy. You should avoid it in the last month. Tylenol, or an analgesic based on acetaminophen, is also recommended for headaches, but be sure to ask your doctor before taking any medication during pregnancy.

I have terrible allergies. Is there anything my doctor is going to be able to recommend?
For some women, pregnancy can feel like a bad head cold. The increased volume of blood to your mucus membranes can make

the lining of your respiratory tract swell. You may even experience nosebleeds. Fortunately, there are safe medications available to ease the symptoms, so consult with your doctor. See about taking extra vitamin C. A humidifier can also be helpful. If you experience nosebleeds as a result of allergies, try packing the nostril with gauze and then pinching your nose between your thumb and forefinger. To shrink the blood vessels and reduce bleeding, try putting an ice pack on your nose.

If I develop an infection, are there any antibiotics safe for expectant moms?

Yes. Pharmaceutical companies are coming up with new antibiotics all the time, and a number of them are safe for pregnancy. Many doctors believe that natural and synthetic penicillins are the safest antibiotics to take during pregnancy, so if you are not allergic to these oldest weapons against infection, you are definitely in luck. If you do get sick, make sure that your obstetrician is aware of anything your family doctor or another specialist may be prescribing.

What are my chances of having twins?

Your chances of "twinning" are actually not bad—about 1 in 90 births result in twins. If fraternal twins run in your family, your odds are slightly higher. The number of twins and multiple births has skyrocketed over the past several decades, and the incidence of higher order multiples—which include triplets, quadruplets, or more—grew a whopping 404 percent between 1980 and 1997, but has experienced a slow but steady decline since 1999. Twins are more common then ever, however, with 119,648 twin births occurring in 2000.

The Centers for Disease Control attributes approximately two-thirds of all U.S. higher order multiples to the use of fertility treatments, also known as assisted reproductive technology (ART). Over 37 percent of all successful pregnancies from ART result in a multiple fraternal birth.

National statistics also reveal that more women are waiting until their thirties and forties to have children, and the increasing twin rate may reflect that reality. Women over 35, especially those who have had a previous multiple birth, have an increased chance of having multiples.

You will have fraternal twins if two separate eggs are fertilized by two separate sperm. Three times more common than identical twins, and based on heredity, these fraternal fetuses have their own placentas, may even be different sexes, and may not look more like each other than ordinary brothers and sisters in the same family.

When a single fertilized egg separates into two distinct halves, identical twins are the result. These unborn babies share the same placenta, are always the same sex, and will have the same genetic makeup and similar physical characteristics.

Carrying two or more babies will put a lot more stress on your body, and your doctor is going to monitor you much more closely than if you were expecting one baby. Early detection of the babies using ultrasounds and by taking blood tests to measure your hormone levels will help keep you on track.

What are the dangers of X-rays to my unborn baby?
According to the American Academy of Family Physicians (AAFP), the maximum safe fetal radiation dose during pregnancy is 5 rad, or the equivalent of 50,000 dental X-rays or 250 mammograms. CT scans, fluoroscopic studies, and nuclear medicine tests involve slightly higher doses than conventional X-rays, but in general still fall well within the range of acceptable exposure. In each case, the benefits of imaging need to be weighed against

the potential risk to the fetus, and if at all possible, tests involving radiation should be avoided in the first trimester of pregnancy.

I have epilepsy and have been seizure-free for several years thanks to my medication. Can I still take my antiepileptic drugs and deliver a healthy baby?
Many obstetricians and pharmacologists get very worried when you mention the words *pregnancy* and *epilepsy* in the same context. However, when you speak to an epileptologist (a doctor specializing in seizure treatment), the news is not all doom and gloom. Andrew Wilner, M.D., of the Neurology Foundation, Providence, RI, and author of *Epilepsy, 199 Answers*, explains, "Although medications can cause birth defects, they usually do not. The risk of birth defects in children to women with epilepsy is about 6 percent. That means there is a 94 percent chance there will be no birth defects."

Dr. Wilner suggests that you sit down with your specialist and plan your pregnancy very carefully, making certain not to begin or stop taking any medications without serious consideration, stating that "the risk of harm to you and your baby is probably greater if you have a convulsion than the risk to your baby from medication." He also explains that pregnancy is a good time to re-evaluate the drugs you may be taking. Your body will be undergoing profound biochemical changes and you may even want to have the drug levels in your blood checked much more frequently than in your recent past. Dr. Wilner maintains that you really want to take "the least number of drugs at the lowest dosages to control your seizures."

Can ultrasounds give misleading information?
While it's possible that you may be having a baby boy even if his external sex organs aren't visible in the ultrasound and therefore

you may incorrectly think you are having a girl, most technicians won't state your baby's gender unless they are absolutely certain. If the sonogram indicates a due date that seems wrong, you might ask, "Could I possibly have dated the start of my pregnancy incorrectly?" Experts say that an ultrasound done at sixteen weeks is more accurate in regards to gestational age than an ultrasound done later in your pregnancy. When dating the length of a pregnancy, the ultrasound technician can be accurate within a few days. Ultrasounds date your pregnancy from the point of conception, which is a few days different from the point of your last period. Later ultrasounds are more accurate when determining your baby's gender. A very clear image must be obtained for the ultrasound to determine whether you are expecting a boy or a girl, and this may be more difficult to see in the early stages.

My dreams seem more vivid now that I'm pregnant. Is there a connection?

Dreams that are exceptionally realistic, disturbing, or just plain bizarre are common in pregnancy. Your dreams are reflections of what's on your mind, so it's natural for them to reflect concerns about the baby, your family, and the future. They may seem larger than life right now due to insecurities about the future and again those pregnancy hormones.

Why do I feel so hot and sweaty?

Your metabolism works overtime during pregnancy. Your body is burning more calories, and as a result, you often feel warm. An increase in blood supply to the surface of your skin, as well as hormones, all have an effect on how hot you feel. Keep cool by dressing in natural fibers and layering clothes so that you can always cool off by removing a layer. Hop in the shower; pat on a little talcum powder afterwards. You may need to change antiperspirants if your normal brand isn't working. To avoid dehydration as your body is working hard to burn calories and produce more blood, drink plenty of water.

Why do I often feel scatterbrained?
Increased hormones can make your thinking a bit foggy—just as they can during your menstrual cycle. Manage the situation by reducing your stress load, making lists, and going easy on yourself.

What is toxoplasmosis, and should I worry about getting it?
Toxoplasmosis is rare, but it is a virus that can affect your baby in the womb. When cats are allowed to run freely outside they can end up with a parasite that settles in the intestines and is passed on through cat feces. Toxoplasmosis can cause brain damage and other medical problems in your unborn child. Cats also frequent gardens and sandboxes, so wear gloves and wash your hands thoroughly after being outside. Don't clean any litter boxes during your pregnancy (ask your partner or a friend to help you).

Can sugar substitutes cause problems during pregnancy?
The Food and Drug Administration and the American Academy of Pediatrics agree that aspartame and saccharin are safe, but unless you have diabetes and need to control your sugar intake, there is no good reason to consume artificial sweeteners. To be safe, limit diet drinks to one a day. However, if you are pregnant and are disgnosed with hyperphenylalanine (high levels of the amino acid phenylalanine—a component of aspartame—in your bloodstream), you should stop using the product immediately, as excessive levels of this amino acid can cause brain damage. People with the genetic disease phenylketonuria (PKU) or advanced liver disease should also avoid aspartame.

My doctor recommends lots of iron, but it makes me feel nauseated. What should I do?

Take iron-rich prenatal vitamin supplements between meals with plenty of water or along with a fruit juice rich in vitamin C, which enhances the absorption of iron. Avoid drinking milk, coffee, or tea with your iron supplements because these beverages inhibit iron absorption. Add liver, red meat, fish, poultry, enriched breads and cereals, green leafy vegetables, eggs, and dried fruits to your diet to increase dietary iron.

What kings of food cravings are normal?

Many pregnant women crave sweet or salty foods. Cravings for non-food items such as dirt, soap, ash, or coffee grounds are different. A phenomenon called pica, which has shown up in medical literature since the sixth century, results in strange cravings that can cause serious problems for a pregnant mother and her unborn baby.

If you have a craving to eat clay, ashes, laundry starch, or other unusual substances, seek medical attention right away.

Can my car's seatbelt harm my unborn baby?

Definitely continue to buckle up throughout your pregnancy. The lap belt should fit snugly under your belly bulge, and the shoulder belt should be positioned between your breasts. Don't worry about your belt putting pressure on your baby. The baby is well protected by amniotic fluid and layers of tissue, muscle, and fat. It's much more dangerous to you and your child to go beltless and risk being injured in an accident.

Does intercourse hurt the baby?

Unless you have a high-risk pregnancy, you are not going to harm your baby by having sex. Sex is quite safe in a normal pregnancy.

Vaginal bleeding, a history of miscarriage or premature labor, or a diagnosis of placental problems are good reasons to restrict intercourse, however. During the last month before your due date, you also should proceed with caution. Ask your practitioner if you have any concerns.

Should I circumcise my baby?

The American Academy of Pediatrics takes the stance that there is currently no firm medical or hygienic ground for performing routine circumcision (removal of the foreskin that covers the head of the penis) in newborn boys. However, the AAP also cited the importance of weighing cultural and religious beliefs and considering the child's best interest when deciding whether or not to circumcise a newborn male. If circumcision is performed, analgesia can be used to relieve the pain.

How soon can I have sex after the baby's birth?

Many doctors recommend waiting four to six weeks before having intercourse. Very few couples are able to swing back into a sex life immediately after the birth of a baby. Keep in mind either way that you can get pregnant in the period following birth. You should get back into your contraceptive routine before the mood strikes. Your doctor can give you a prescription before you leave the hospital, if necessary.

I can't stand wearing my favorite perfume anymore! Can pregnancy cause your nose to go haywire?

Pregnancy causes a heightened sensitivity to certain odors—coffee, cigarette smoke, and fried food are frequent offenders—that can contribute to stomach unrest. One theory is that these olfactory aversions are your body's way of keeping you away from substances that could harm your developing baby.

Will coloring my hair hurt my baby?

To date, there is no conclusive evidence that hair color use in pregnancy is dangerous. If you are concerned over a possible risk, you may opt for a vegetable-based or temporary color treatment until your baby is born. Some experts also recommend holding off on all chemical hair treatments during the first trimester.

I'm getting varicose veins in my legs. Is this common in pregnancy?

The hair-fine marks, also known as spider veins, usually appear on the lower legs and are caused when increased blood volume and pressure damage the valves that regulate blood flow up out of the blood vessels of the legs. The result is pooled blood in the vein and that telltale squiggly red or blue line.

Supportive stockings, putting your feet up, resting on your left side, and taking an occasional walk when you need to stand for long periods of time may relieve leg soreness associated with varicose veins.

I've had a miscarriage in the past. Is there a way to prevent it this time around?

Many miscarriages occur due to factors completely beyond anyone's control—a defective egg or sperm, or implantation outside of the endometrium. Other triggers, such as teratogen exposure, may be avoided with special precautions in pregnancy. Speak with your healthcare provider about your concerns and any special instructions given your medical history (such as restrictions on your activity).

What if I don't get to the hospital in time?

Every woman has heard stories of impatient babies being born in the backseats of taxicabs, but these impromptu deliveries are not common. Most women have plenty of time to make it to the hospital safe and sound; the average labor period runs 12 to 14 hours. If you're concerned, you can take some basic precautions. Work out a route to the hospital in advance with your partner, keep your gas tank full, and have cash on hand for a cab just in case your car chooses the moment you go into labor to conk out.

If I'm overdue, will my provider induce me if I request it?

Whether or not to induce depends on a number of factors. Is the cervix effaced or dilated? Are you fairly sure your due date was accurate to begin with? Have you had a previous C-section? Generally, if you've hit the 41-week-mark, you have no history of C-section, and your provider thinks induction is indicated, she will schedule one for you.

What is umbilical cord banking?

The umbilical cord blood contains stem cells, those blank slate cells from which all organs and tissues are built. Cord blood collected immediately after birth is placed in a collection kit and flown to a facility where it is cryogenically frozen and "banked" for later use if needed. The theory behind cord banking is that if your child ever develops a disease or condition requiring stem-cell treatment, the cord blood can be thawed and used for her treatment. If it matches certain biological markers, cord blood can be used to treat other family members as well. However, banking is cost-prohibitive for many and requires an annual storage fee for as long as you would like the cord blood frozen.

I have splotches of discolored skin on my face and abdomen. Is this normal?

Yes. Pregnancy hormones can cause hyperpigmentation of your skin, which makes certain areas of your skin (most commonly around the forehead, nose, cheeks, abdomen, and areolas) to darken. These discolored spots are usually dark on light-skinned women and light on dark-skinned women. Don't worry, though— these discolored patches will fade and eventually go away after your baby is born.

Are there exercises I should avoid during pregnancy?
Yes. A few sports are considered inappropriate during any phase of pregnancy. Mostly these sports are dangerous for reasons related to balance and risk of physical blows. It is not recommended that pregnant women ride horses, scuba dive, downhill ski, play rugby, or engage in other contact sports.

How do I know if I'm doing Kegel exercises right?
If you are doing Kegels correctly, you will not be tightening other muscles like your buttocks or thighs. You will be isolating this internal muscle and not straining other ones in the process.

Can I raise my arms above my head while pregnant?
There is an old wives' tale that says if you are pregnant, you should not lift your arms over your head. In doing so, the myth goes, you will cause your baby's umbilical cord to wrap around its neck. This is utter nonsense and should not affect how you work your arms out or move during pregnancy.

Will eating too much sugar during pregnancy lead to gestational diabetes?
No, eating too much sugar does not directly cause any type of diabetes. Diabetes is a disorder in which the body cannot properly utilize insulin or does not produce insulin, which regulates blood sugar levels. Gestational diabetes is the result of changing hormones within a woman's body.

Do folic acid supplements really make that much of a difference in preventing certain birth defects?
According to the United States Centers for Disease Control (CDC), when taken one month before conception and throughout the first trimester, folic acid supplements have been proven to reduce the risk for an NTD-affected pregnancy by 50 to 70 percent.

Can eating more than three times a day be part of a healthy diet?
Yes. For women who are pregnant or for anybody who enjoys a healthy lifestyle, eating several small meals during the day can fit nicely into a healthy eating pattern. It can help you to fit in those extra calories and food group servings without having to eat large meals all at once, which can be difficult for women who may be having a problem with nausea or morning sickness.

Is it OK to take a calcium supplement if I don't eat dairy foods?
If you can't get enough calcium from the foods you choose, a supplement can be a good idea. The rule of thumb should always be food before supplements, though. First, include calcium-containing foods in your diet as much as possible, and then supplement on top of that. Never let a supplement take the place of an entire food group or nutrient such as calcium.

When should I call my doctor about a headache?
If you are in your second or third trimester and experience a bad headache, or a headache for the first time during your pregnancy, you should contact your doctor. If you have a severe headache that comes on suddenly, won't go away, and is unlike any you have ever experienced, you should call your doctor. You should contact your doctor if you have a headache that worsens and is accompanied by vision problems, speech problems, drowsiness, and/or numbness.

Also call your doctor if your headache is accompanied by a stiff neck and fever.

Is it unhealthy to have an aversion to vegetables during my first trimester?
It is common for women to have food aversions even to healthy foods such as vegetables. Try drinking vegetable juice instead of eating whole vegetables. You can also eat more fruit, since many of them contain some of the same nutrients as vegetables. Keep taking your prenatal vitamins to ensure you are getting all of the nutrients that your body needs at this time. However, it's always best to get your nutrients from food before supplements. If you have a temporary aversion to a healthy food, make substitutions. If you're not sure what to substitute, be sure to speak to a dietitian.

How can I tell whether I am experiencing morning sickness or something more serious?
If you vomit more than three or four times a day, are hardly able to keep any food down, lose weight, feel very tired and dizzy, and urinate less than usual, you may have something more serious than run-of-the-mill morning sickness—specifically, you may be suffering from hyperemesis gravidarum (HG). Additional symptoms include increased heart rate, headaches, and pale, dry-looking skin. It is important to diagnose and treat HG as soon as possible, so contact your doctor if you feel any of these symptoms or feel that your morning sickness is more serious.

Appendix B
Important Contact Information

Insurance Company

Company name:
....

Policy number:
....

Phone number:
....

Address:
....

....

Office hours:
....

E-mail address:
....

Family Doctor

Name:
....

Office phone number:
....

Emergency phone number:
....

Office address:
....

....

Office hours:
....

E-mail address:
....

Gynecologist

Name:
....

Office phone number:
....

Emergency phone number:
....

Office address:
....

....

Office hours:
....

E-mail address:
....

Obstetrician

Name:
....

Office phone number:
....

Emergency phone number:
....

Office address:
....

....

Office hours:
....

E-mail address:
....

Midwife

Name:
....

Office phone number:
....

Emergency phone number:
....

Office address:
....

....

Available hours:
....

E-mail address:
....

Doula

Name:
....

Office phone number:
....

Emergency phone number:
....

Office address:
....

....

Available hours:
....

E-mail address:
....

Hospital

Name:
....

Phone number:
....

Emergency phone number:
....

Address:
....

....

Visiting hours:
....

E-mail address:
....

Pediatrician

Name:
....

Office phone number:
....

Emergency phone number:
....

Office address:
....

....

Office hours:
....

E-mail address:
....

Name:
....

Phone number:
....

Emergency phone number:
....

Address:
....

....

E-mail address:
....

Name:
....

Phone number:
....

Emergency phone number:
....

Address:
....

....

E-mail address:
....

Name:
....

Phone number:
....

Emergency phone number:
....

Address:
....

....

E-mail address:
....

Name:
....

Phone number:
....

Emergency phone number:
....

Address:
....

....

E-mail address:
....

Name:
....

Phone number:
....

Emergency phone number:
....

Address:
....

....

E-mail address:
....

Name:
....

Phone number:
....

Emergency phone number:
....

Address:
....

....

E-mail address:
....

Name:
....

Phone number:
....

Emergency phone number:
....

Address:
....

....

E-mail address:
....

Name:
....

Phone number:
....

Emergency phone number:
....

Address:
....

....

E-mail address:
....

Name:
....

Phone number:
....

Emergency phone number:
....

Address:
....

....

E-mail address:
....

Name:
....

Phone number:
....

Emergency phone number:
....

Address:
....

....

E-mail address:
....

Name:
....

Phone number:
....

Emergency phone number:
....

Address:
....

....

E-mail address:
....

Name:
....

Phone number:
....

Emergency phone number:
....

Address:
....

....

E-mail address:
....

Name:
....

Phone number:
....

Emergency phone number:
....

Address:
....

....

E-mail address:
....

Name:
....

Phone number:
....

Emergency phone number:
....

Address:
....

....

E-mail address:
....

Name:
....

Phone number:
....

Emergency phone number:
....

Address:
....

....

E-mail address:
....

Name:
....

Phone number:
....

Emergency phone number:
....

Address:
....

....

E-mail address:
....

Name:
....

Phone number:
....

Emergency phone number:
....

Address:
....

....

E-mail address:
....

Name:
....

Phone number:
....

Emergency phone number:
....

Address:
....

....

E-mail address:
....

Name:
....

Phone number:
....

Emergency phone number:
....

Address:
....

....

E-mail address:
....

Name:
....

Phone number:
....

Emergency phone number:
....

Address:
....

....

E-mail address:
....

Name:
....

Phone number:
....

Emergency phone number:
....

Address:
....

....

E-mail address:
....

Name:
....

Phone number:
....

Emergency phone number:
....

Address:
....

....

E-mail address:
....

Name:
....

Phone number:
....

Emergency phone number:
....

Address:
....

....

E-mail address:
....

Name:
....

Phone number:
....

Emergency phone number:
....

Address:
....

....

E-mail address:
....

Name:
....

Phone number:
....

Emergency phone number:
....

Address:
....

....

E-mail address:
....

Name:
....

Phone number:
....

Emergency phone number:
....

Address:
....

....

E-mail address:
....

Name:
....

Phone number:
....

Emergency phone number:
....

Address:
....

....

E-mail address:
....

Name:
....

Phone number:
....

Emergency phone number:
....

Address:
....

....

E-mail address:
....

Name:
....

Phone number:
....

Emergency phone number:
....

Address:
....

....

E-mail address:
....

Name:
....

Phone number:
....

Emergency phone number:
....

Address:
....

....

E-mail address:
....

Name:
....

Phone number:
....

Emergency phone number:
....

Address:
....

....

E-mail address:
....

Name:
....

Phone number:
....

Emergency phone number:
....

Address:
....

....

E-mail address:
....

Name:
....

Phone number:
....

Emergency phone number:
....

Address:
....

....

E-mail address:
....

Ten Month
Calendar

Appendix C
Ten Month Calendar

_____   _____
Month   _Week_

Monday

Tuesday

Wednesday

Thursday

Friday

Saturday   Sunday

Month

Week

Monday

Tuesday

Wednesday

Thursday

Friday

Saturday

Sunday

Month

Week

Monday

Tuesday

Wednesday

Thursday

Friday

Saturday

Sunday

Month

Week

Monday

Tuesday

Wednesday

Thursday

Friday

Saturday

Sunday

Month

Week

Monday

Tuesday

Wednesday

Thursday

Friday

Saturday

Sunday

Month

Week

Monday

Tuesday

Wednesday

Thursday

Friday

Saturday

Sunday

Month _Week_

○ Monday

○ Tuesday

○ Wednesday

○ Thursday

○ Friday

○ Saturday

○ Sunday

Monday

Tuesday

Wednesday

Thursday

Friday

Saturday

Sunday

_____   _____
Month   *Week*

Monday

Tuesday

Wednesday

Thursday

Friday

Saturday   Sunday

Month

Week

Monday

Tuesday

Wednesday

Thursday

Friday

Saturday

Sunday

Month

Week

Monday

Tuesday

Wednesday

Thursday

Friday

Saturday

Sunday

Month

Week

Monday

Tuesday

Wednesday

Thursday

Friday

Saturday

Sunday

Month

Week

Monday

Tuesday

Wednesday

Thursday

Friday

Saturday

Sunday

Month

Week

Monday

Tuesday

Wednesday

Thursday

Friday

Saturday

Sunday

Monday

Tuesday

Wednesday

Thursday

Friday

Saturday

Sunday

Month

Week

Monday

Tuesday

Wednesday

Thursday

Friday

Saturday

Sunday

Month   _Week_

○ Monday

○ Tuesday

○ Wednesday

○ Thursday

○ Friday

○ Saturday   ○ Sunday

Month _Week_

Monday

Tuesday

Wednesday

Thursday

Friday

Saturday

Sunday

Month

Week

Monday

Tuesday

Wednesday

Thursday

Friday

Saturday

Sunday

Monday

Tuesday

Wednesday

Thursday

Friday

Saturday

Sunday

Month

Week

○ Monday

○ Tuesday

○ Wednesday

○ Thursday

○ Friday

○ Saturday

○ Sunday

Monday

Tuesday

Wednesday

Thursday

Friday

Saturday

Sunday

Monday

Tuesday

Wednesday

Thursday

Friday

Saturday

Sunday

Month

Week

Monday

Tuesday

Wednesday

Thursday

Friday

Saturday

Sunday

Month

Week

Monday

Tuesday

Wednesday

Thursday

Friday

Saturday

Sunday

Monday

Tuesday

Wednesday

Thursday

Friday

Saturday

Sunday

Month

Week

Monday

Tuesday

Wednesday

Thursday

Friday

Saturday

Sunday

Month

Week

Monday

Tuesday

Wednesday

Thursday

Friday

Saturday

Sunday

[275]

Month

Week

○ Monday

○ Tuesday

○ Wednesday

○ Thursday

○ Friday

○ Saturday

○ Sunday

Month

Week

Monday

Tuesday

Wednesday

Thursday

Friday

Saturday

Sunday

Month

Week

Monday

Tuesday

Wednesday

Thursday

Friday

Saturday

Sunday

Monday

Tuesday

Wednesday

Thursday

Friday

Saturday

Sunday

Month

Week

Monday

Tuesday

Wednesday

Thursday

Friday

Saturday

Sunday

Month

Week

Monday

Tuesday

Wednesday

Thursday

Friday

Saturday

Sunday

Month

Week

Monday

Tuesday

Wednesday

Thursday

Friday

Saturday

Sunday

Month

Week

Monday

Tuesday

Wednesday

Thursday

Friday

Saturday

Sunday

Month _Week_

Monday

Tuesday

Wednesday

Thursday

Friday

Saturday

Sunday

Month

Week

Monday

Tuesday

Wednesday

Thursday

Friday

Saturday

Sunday

Monday

Tuesday

Wednesday

Thursday

Friday

Saturday

Sunday

Month

Week

Monday

Tuesday

Wednesday

Thursday

Friday

Saturday

Sunday

Appendix D

Estimated Due Date Table

This chart lists due dates by month. Find the month and date on which your last menstrual period began, then look to the right of that line to see what your estimated due date is.

Estimated Due Date Table

DATE OF LAST PERIOD	YOUR EDD	DATE OF LAST PERIOD	YOUR EDD
1/1	10/8	2/7	11/14
1/2	10/9	2/8	11/15
1/3	10/10	2/9	11/16
1/4	10/11	2/10	11/17
1/5	10/12	2/11	11/18
1/6	10/13	2/12	11/19
1/7	10/14	2/13	11/20
1/8	10/15	2/14	11/21
1/9	10/16	2/15	11/22
1/10	10/17	2/16	11/23
1/11	10/18	2/17	11/24
1/12	10/19	2/18	11/25
1/13	10/20	2/19	11/26
1/14	10/21	2/20	11/27
1/15	10/22	2/21	11/28
1/16	10/23	2/22	11/29
1/17	10/24	2/23	11/30
1/18	10/25	2/24	12/1
1/19	10/26	2/25	12/2
1/20	10/27	2/26	12/3
1/21	10/28	2/27	12/4
1/22	10/29	2/28	12/5
1/23	10/30	**3/1**	12/6
1/24	10/31	3/2	12/7
1/25	11/1	3/3	12/8
1/26	11/2	3/4	12/9
1/27	11/3	3/5	12/10
1/28	11/4	3/6	12/11
1/29	11/5	3/7	12/12
1/30	11/6	3/8	12/13
1/31	11/7	3/9	12/14
2/1	11/8	3/10	12/15
2/2	11/9	3/11	12/16
2/3	11/10	3/12	12/17
2/4	11/11	3/13	12/18
2/5	11/12	3/14	12/19
2/6	11/13	3/15	12/20

Estimated Due Date Table

DATE OF LAST PERIOD	YOUR EDD	DATE OF LAST PERIOD	YOUR EDD
3/16	12/21	4/22	1/27
3/17	12/22	4/23	1/28
3/18	12/23	4/24	1/29
3/19	12/24	4/25	1/30
3/20	12/25	4/26	1/31
3/21	12/26	4/27	2/1
3/22	12/27	4/28	2/2
3/23	12/28	4/29	2/3
3/24	12/29	4/30	2/4
3/25	12/30	**5/1**	2/5
3/26	12/31	5/2	2/6
3/27	1/1	5/3	2/7
3/28	1/2	5/4	2/8
3/29	1/3	5/5	2/9
3/30	1/4	5/6	2/10
3/31	1/5	5/7	2/11
4/1	1/6	5/8	2/12
4/2	1/7	5/9	2/13
4/3	1/8	5/10	2/14
4/4	1/9	5/11	2/15
4/5	1/10	5/12	2/16
4/6	1/11	5/13	2/17
4/7	1/12	5/14	2/18
4/8	1/13	5/15	2/19
4/9	1/14	5/16	2/20
4/10	1/15	5/17	2/21
4/11	1/16	5/18	2/22
4/12	1/17	5/19	2/23
4/13	1/18	5/20	2/24
4/14	1/19	5/21	2/25
4/15	1/20	5/22	2/26
4/16	1/21	5/23	2/27
4/17	1/22	5/24	2/28
4/18	1/23	5/25	3/1
4/19	1/24	5/26	3/2
4/20	1/25	5/27	3/3
4/21	1/26	5/28	3/4

Estimated Due Date Table

DATE OF LAST PERIOD	YOUR EDD	DATE OF LAST PERIOD	YOUR EDD
5/29	3/5	7/5	4/11
5/30	3/6	7/6	4/12
5/31	3/7	7/7	4/13
6/1	3/8	7/8	4/14
6/2	3/9	7/9	4/15
6/3	3/10	7/10	4/16
6/4	3/11	7/11	4/17
6/5	3/12	7/12	4/18
6/6	3/13	7/13	4/19
6/7	3/14	7/14	4/20
6/8	3/15	7/15	4/21
6/9	3/16	7/16	4/22
6/10	3/17	7/17	4/23
6/11	3/18	7/18	4/24
6/12	3/19	7/19	4/25
6/13	3/20	7/20	4/26
6/14	3/21	7/21	4/27
6/15	3/22	7/22	4/28
6/16	3/23	7/23	4/29
6/17	3/24	7/24	4/30
6/18	3/25	7/25	5/1
6/19	3/26	7/26	5/2
6/20	3/27	7/27	5/3
6/21	3/28	7/28	5/4
6/22	3/29	7/29	5/5
6/23	3/30	7/30	5/6
6/24	3/31	7/31	5/7
6/25	4/1	**8/1**	5/8
6/26	4/2	8/2	5/9
6/27	4/3	8/3	5/10
6/28	4/4	8/4	5/11
6/29	4/5	8/5	5/12
6/30	4/6	8/6	5/13
7/1	4/7	8/7	5/14
7/2	4/8	8/8	5/15
7/3	4/9	8/9	5/16
7/4	4/10	8/10	5/17

Estimated Due Date Table

DATE OF LAST PERIOD	YOUR EDD	DATE OF LAST PERIOD	YOUR EDD
8/11	5/18	9/17	6/24
8/12	5/19	9/18	6/25
8/13	5/20	9/19	6/26
8/14	5/21	9/20	6/27
8/15	5/22	9/21	6/28
8/16	5/23	9/22	6/29
8/17	5/24	9/23	6/30
8/18	5/25	9/24	7/1
8/19	5/26	9/25	7/2
8/20	5/27	9/26	7/3
8/21	5/28	9/27	7/4
8/22	5/29	9/28	7/5
8/23	5/30	9/29	7/6
8/24	5/31	9/30	7/7
8/25	6/1	**10/1**	7/8
8/26	6/2	10/2	7/9
8/27	6/3	10/3	7/10
8/28	6/4	10/4	7/11
8/29	6/5	10/5	7/12
8/30	6/6	10/6	7/13
8/31	6/7	10/7	7/14
9/1	6/8	10/8	7/15
9/2	6/9	10/9	7/16
9/3	6/10	10/10	7/17
9/4	6/11	10/11	7/18
9/5	6/12	10/12	7/19
9/6	6/13	10/13	7/20
9/7	6/14	10/14	7/21
9/8	6/15	10/15	7/22
9/9	6/16	10/16	7/23
9/10	6/17	10/17	7/24
9/11	6/18	10/18	7/25
9/12	6/19	10/19	7/26
9/13	6/20	10/20	7/27
9/14	6/21	10/21	7/28
9/15	6/22	10/22	7/29
9/16	6/23	10/23	7/30

Estimated Due Date Table

DATE OF LAST PERIOD	YOUR EDD	DATE OF LAST PERIOD	YOUR EDD
10/24	7/31	11/28	9/4
10/25	8/1	11/29	9/5
10/26	8/2	11/30	9/6
10/27	8/3	**12/1**	9/7
10/28	8/4	12/2	9/8
10/29	8/5	12/3	9/9
10/30	8/6	12/4	9/10
10/31	8/7	12/5	9/11
11/1	8/8	12/6	9/12
11/2	8/9	12/7	9/13
11/3	8/10	12/8	9/14
11/4	8/11	12/9	9/15
11/5	8/12	12/10	9/16
11/6	8/13	12/11	9/17
11/7	8/14	12/12	9/18
11/8	8/15	12/13	9/19
11/9	8/16	12/14	9/20
11/10	8/17	12/15	9/21
11/11	8/18	12/16	9/22
11/12	8/19	12/17	9/23
11/13	8/20	12/18	9/24
11/14	8/21	12/19	9/25
11/15	8/22	12/20	9/26
11/16	8/23	12/21	9/27
11/17	8/24	12/22	9/28
11/18	8/25	12/23	9/29
11/19	8/26	12/24	9/30
11/20	8/27	12/25	10/1
11/21	8/28	12/26	10/2
11/22	8/29	12/27	10/3
11/23	8/30	12/28	10/4
11/24	8/31	12/29	10/5
11/25	9/1	12/30	10/6
11/26	9/2	12/31	10/7
11/27	9/3		